Anglo-Saxons

A Captivating Guide to the People Who Inhabited Great Britain from the Early Middle Ages to the Norman Conquest of England

© **Copyright 2019**

All Rights Reserved. No part of this book may be reproduced in any form without permission in writing from the author. Reviewers may quote brief passages in reviews.

Disclaimer: No part of this publication may be reproduced or transmitted in any form or by any means, mechanical or electronic, including photocopying or recording, or by any information storage and retrieval system, or transmitted by email without permission in writing from the publisher.

While all attempts have been made to verify the information provided in this publication, neither the author nor the publisher assumes any responsibility for errors, omissions or contrary interpretations of the subject matter herein.

This book is for entertainment purposes only. The views expressed are those of the author alone, and should not be taken as expert instruction or commands. The reader is responsible for his or her own actions.

Adherence to all applicable laws and regulations, including international, federal, state and local laws governing professional licensing, business practices, advertising and all other aspects of doing business in the US, Canada, UK or any other jurisdiction is the sole responsibility of the purchaser or reader.

Neither the author nor the publisher assumes any responsibility or liability whatsoever on the behalf of the purchaser or reader of these materials. Any perceived slight of any individual or organization is purely unintentional.

Free Bonus from Captivating History (Available for a Limited time)

Hi History Lovers!

Now you have a chance to join our exclusive history list so you can get your first history ebook for free as well as discounts and a potential to get more history books for free! Simply visit the link below to join.

Captivatinghistory.com/ebook

Also, make sure to follow us on Facebook, Twitter and Youtube by searching for Captivating History.

Contents

INTRODUCTION 1

CHAPTER 1 – ANGLO-SAXONS ARRIVE 3

    Roman Britain 4

    Sub-Roman Britain 8

CHAPTER 2 – EARLY ANGLO-SAXONS: ORIGINS AND PRE-SETTLEMENT HISTORY 11

CHAPTER 3 – THE CULTURE OF ANGLO-SAXONS: RELIGION, CUSTOMS, SOCIAL HIERARCHY, EARLY CHRISTIANITY 16

    Religion of the Anglo-Saxons 16

    Anglo-Saxon Customs 20

    Social Structure of the Anglo-Saxons 24

    Early Christianity 29

CHAPTER 4 – EVERYDAY LIFE OF ANGLO-SAXON ENGLAND: JOBS AND DIVISION OF LABOR, FOOD AND DRINK, CLOTHES, ARCHITECTURE, TRAVEL, WARS, GENDER AND AGE NORMS, ART, WRITTEN WORKS 32

    Jobs and Division of Labor 32

    Food and Drink 35

    Clothes 37

    Anglo-Saxon Architecture 38

    Travel 43

WARS	46
GENDER AND AGE NORMS	51
ANGLO-SAXON ART	54
WRITTEN WORKS OF THE ANGLO-SAXON PERIOD	59
CHAPTER 5 – ANGLO-SAXON KINGDOMS	**63**
BEFORE THE KINGS	63
THE TRIBAL HIDAGE	64
BRETWALDA	67
LIST OF KINGDOMS	68
EAST ANGLIA	68
Notable East Anglian Kings	*70*
Other Notable Kings of East Anglia	*72*
KENT	73
Notable Kings of Kent	*74*
Other Notable Kings of Kent	*78*
ESSEX	78
Notable kings of Essex	*79*
Other Notable Kings of Essex	*81*
SUSSEX	82
Notable Kings of Sussex	*83*
Other Notable Kings of Sussex	*84*
NORTHUMBRIA	85
Notable Northumbrian Kings	*86*
Other Notable Kings of Northumbria	*91*
MERCIA	91
Notable Kings of Mercia	*92*
Other Notable Kings of Mercia	*96*
WESSEX	97
Notable Kings of Wessex	*97*

Other Notable Kings of Wessex *103*
CHAPTER 6 – ANGLO-SAXON LEGACY **105**
CONCLUSION **108**
BIBLIOGRAPHY AND REFERENCES..**111**
NOTES ON IMAGES **113**

Introduction

At one point in our history, the United Kingdom was the dominant force on the planet. They had roughly a quarter of the world's land and a quarter of the world's population under their direct control. The queen was the most powerful monarch alive, and even if we look at Queen Elizabeth today, we can safely say that she's a strong political figure simply by virtue of existing and ruling the kingdom.

However, the United Kingdom is fairly young, historically speaking. Before it saw the union between Britain and Ireland (which would later secede, though without its northern part), the kingdom had to be united itself. Even today, Scotland, Wales, and England are considered separate countries, despite not really being independent and the Crown presiding over all three.

Yet, there was a time even before that, before even England was united. This was a time before William the Bastard decided to prove to his contemporaries that his bastard moniker would be erased with a swift conquest of the biggest island northwest of Europe. A time before the Battle of Hastings and the year 1066. A time when many petty kingdoms ruled, conquered, and were liberated, time and time again, by a specific people group. A people group that is, in fact, a blend of many and that authors of later dates would collectively call the Anglo-Saxons.

With this book, we want to let our readers know how vibrant and lively (as well as deadly) life in Britain was during the perhaps wrongly-titled "Dark Ages." With the end of the Roman Empire, the local Britons were left to their devices, and it would be several people groups from a peninsula in Central Europe that would come to dominate the island, making sure their presence was known through a series of kingdoms, battles, clashes, victories, and defeats. But the Anglo-Saxons have a lot more to offer us history buffs. We can learn about their day-to-day life: how they dressed, what they ate and drank, how they waged war or had fun, how they buried their dead, and how they worshiped their gods. We can also learn about their art, their amazing metal and clay pieces, stunning bits of tapestries, and dozens of well-illuminated manuscripts. And if we lack any information on what they thought of the world around them, we can be happy that they were willing to tell us that themselves, all through hundreds of written texts of both religious and secular nature.

The Anglo-Saxons were, indeed, an odd group of people to take control of Britain. But they didn't do it all at once, and just like any other people in history, they had a period of adjustment, growth, reconstruction, and eventual rise to prominence. And it all had to start at the same place their British predecessors left off.

Chapter 1 – Anglo-Saxons Arrive

The history of Britain, in general, has always been one of different people groups conquering, mixing, adapting, and evolving. Before the advent of the United Kingdom, nearly every legal (or rather, regal) power has been in the hands of an outsider. Even if we take the earliest history of the isle, we can see that the central power belonged to a nation—Romans, Anglo-Saxons, Normans—that unequivocally came from the continent. And nearly every time they took hold of the isle, the culture would shift.

Possibly the best way to illustrate how this worked is to use an example not from history but from fiction. Author George R. R. Martin, himself a big history buff, drew a lot of inspiration for his works from the ancient and medieval history of the world, with a special focus on European and, specifically, British history.

In Martin's *A Song of Ice and Fire* series, most of the plot is set in the continent of Westeros. Let's sum up the history of this fictional continent for a moment. The first people that lived there were the Children of the Forest, an allusion to elves. But then the First Men came, wars were waged, pacts were sealed, and the First Men even adopted some of the Children's customs as their own. A little later, different invaders known as Andals struck the continent and assumed command. They mixed with the local populace, and little by little, they replaced most of the First Men but not all of them, as those in the North retained the culture of celebrating the Children's

Old Gods. The Andals formed royal houses, and each of them vied for power. However, they were almost all crushed by Aegon the Conqueror who (almost) united the continent and was declared king of the Seven Kingdoms.

So, why bring up a piece of fiction in a history book? Well, because, aside from drawing some inspiration from other bits of fiction, Martin based this whole story on the early history of Britain. Westeros is clearly the island of Great Britain, and the Children have some basis in the old Celtic people that inhabited the isle. Their Old Gods are also inspired by Celtic deities with their own links to nature, forests, and meadows. The First Men could be a good allegory for the Romans, and the Andals of the story are more than likely based on one of the many Germanic people groups that invaded the isle after the decline of the Romans. By the very name, you can tell that they represent the Angles. Another twist by Martin is that his Andals brought the Religion of the Seven with them, an allegory for Christianity. Of course, in reality, this wasn't done by Angles but rather by the Romans before them. Angles, Saxons, and Jutes merely established their own dioceses and took control of the clergy bit by bit. Historically speaking, Angles, much like Martin's Andals, interbred with the locals, formed their own kingdoms, and fought for supremacy. And then we get to Aegon, who is very clearly based on William the Conqueror of Normandy. William gradually took control of the isle in 1066, after the famous Battle of Hastings, starting a new chapter in the history of Britain, once again under foreign rule.

We can see here that authors like Martin found the history of these people fascinating enough to reimagine in their fictional settings. But for now, let's focus on the history of Great Britain before and during the arrival of Germanic tribes from Central Europe.

Roman Britain

As early as 43 CE, Romans established military and political control over most of Britain. The only area they couldn't take was what today comprises Scotland, which at the time was ruled over by the so-called Caledonians. In fact, the famous Hadrian's Wall, built in 128 CE, as well as the later Antonine Wall (construction began around 142 CE and took a little over a decade to complete) were put up as countermeasures against the constant Caledonian attacks.

Roman citizens from all over the empire would come to inhabit the isle. Public and private buildings were steadily rising, and the Britons got sturdy Roman roads. While there weren't any "high-profile" centers of power in Roman Britain, some high officials nevertheless called the isle their home.

During the late Roman period, or more specifically during the Diocletian reforms in 296, the island was divided into four provinces called collectively the Diocese of the Britons. These four were called Britannia Prima, Britannia Secunda, Flavia Caesariensis, and Maxima Caesariensis. However, in the 5th century, an additional province, Valentia, was formed between the two great walls of the north. A vicarius (better known as vicar in English) was in charge of the diocese with his center being in Londinium, though some researchers note that this speculation has its own flaws.

Map of Roman Britannia c. 410[i]

With the decline of the Roman Empire, the ruling Romans paid less and less attention to Britain. The Roman Empire had already been all but divided in the late 3rd and early 4th centuries CE, and the constant incursions by various barbarian tribes, alongside political intrigue and internal conflict, kept the emperors busy on the continent. On occasion, some political figure would emerge and stir up some trouble on the isle, but it would be over in a matter of years.

Historians usually mention the year 410 as the year Roman rule officially ended in Britain. Of course, the whole story is a bit more complex than that. For example, there's the period between 383 and 388 CE when Britain was "ruled" by the Roman general Magnus Maximus. He was appointed general of the isle before this period but had killed the Western Roman emperor Gratian and proclaimed himself a Caesar (or a sub-emperor) of Gaul and Britain, subservient only to Emperor Theodosius, the last emperor to rule over both halves of the ailing empire. During this time, he had to deal with the Picts, originally from the territory of today's Scotland, and the Scoti of Ireland who were invading the isle, as well as with the Saxons, one of the tribes that will come to populate the isle a century or so later. There's a strong possibility that Maximus even appointed local tribe leaders into key political positions. It was also during his reign, according to a few written sources (most notably Gildas), that he moved most of his troops from Hadrian's Wall to the continent in order to pursue his campaigns there. He was beaten at the Battle of the Save and later at the Battle of Poetovio after an unsuccessful bid to claim eastern parts of the empire. Theodosius himself executed him in 388.

Before Theodosius himself passed away in 395, he had to quell another rebellion by Eugenius, a usurper claiming the western part of the empire for himself. After his death, Theodosius' sons ruled as emperors of two distinct "countries," with the western part governed by Honorius and the eastern part by Arcadius. Neither ruler proved to be a capable monarch.

Before Honorius came of age, his father-in-law Stilicho did the bulk of the work keeping the Western Roman Empire together. During this time, raids by outside tribes increased to the point of Stilicho allegedly initiating a war campaign against the Picts, possibly in 398. Mere years later, roughly around 401, he had to withdraw troops from Hadrian's Wall in order to deal with Ostrogoths and Visigoths on the continent. The year 402 is the last year Britain saw a major influx of Roman coins, suggesting that the empire had no financial power to retain the island and defend it properly. Picts, Scoti, and Saxons raided far more than earlier, and the locals had no real means of defense with the Roman generals gone.

The last time any Roman noble would provide any significant change in Britain was in 407. Less than a year earlier, several tribes, including the Suebi, the Alans, and the Vandals, crossed the river Rhine. Britain's Roman soldiers were few and far between, and with the news of barbaric tribes crossing the river, they rallied to defend the isle from a possible invasion. Constantine III, a soldier, was chosen as their leader, and shortly after, he declared himself emperor and crossed the English Channel to look for support in Gaul. The current Western Roman emperor, the now adult Honorius, had to deal with the Visigoth threat, so he had no manpower nor time to deal with Constantine. This gave the leader of the British Romans an opportunity to extend his rule over the territory belonging to today's Spain. However, his rule would prove to be a short one. As early as 409, his troops began to desert him, favoring Honorius. In addition, the continental Saxons were raiding Gaul at an alarmingly increasing rate. Constantine's son and other loyalists were murdered soon after, and in 411, Constantine III was assassinated.

Before any of this happened, however, Emperor Honorius suffered a major defeat. Namely, in 410, the Visigoths sacked Rome, which was the first time any outside power had taken the city in nearly eight centuries. Of course, the royal court had long since moved to Ravenna, but this sacking was nevertheless a shock to the world at the time. During the same year, the local Britons allegedly asked Honorius to assist them with the barbarian raids which had only increased since the time of Magnus Maximus. In a response called the Rescript of Honorius, the emperor supposedly told the locals to defend themselves as he was obviously preoccupied with defending continental Roman lands. Some historians speculate that he didn't write the Rescript for the people of Britain but rather for the people of Bruttium in Italy, known today as the region of Calabria. Whatever the case, the political events in the Western Roman Empire left it unable to defend Britain, hence why the date of 410 usually marks the definite end of Roman rule on the island.

Sub-Roman Britain

Normally, people think that 410 is the year when everything Roman ended with Britain, as it was no longer part of the empire. However, it's far more likely, even without any written or archeological evidence, that Roman culture lingered for a few decades longer.

One key element of the Roman culture that survived in Britain was religion. In fact, mass was conducted in Latin, and most literary sources we have from this period point to Latin still being the language of the Church. Most written sources from the sub-Roman period of Britain come to us from churches, written and collected by men of the cloth. Gildas' *De Excidio et Conquestu Britanniae* (On the Ruin and Conquest of Britain) is possibly the best-known work from this time period, with the Venerable Bede's *Historia ecclesiastica gentis Anglorum* (Ecclesiastical History of the English People) coming roughly two centuries later. Namely, Gildas probably wrote his work in the early 6th century, whereas Bede's *Historia* came out around 731 CE. That would make the former of the two a closer "contemporary" to what we call sub-Roman Britain, even though there's a gap of at least one century between Gildas writing his work and the Romans abandoning Britain entirely.

Most scholars see Gildas' work as not completely reliable. This is because it wasn't written as a historical overview of contemporary Britain but rather as a sermon where the priest condemns the actions of the people living on the isle. However, if some of his descriptions are to be believed, sub-Roman Britain thrived (to some extent, at least) without direct Roman jurisdiction. The people were likely engaged in rebuilding projects, most of which included work on sewage systems and even new Roman-style baths. This much can also be extrapolated from actual archeological data. People still retained Roman law, and the clergy spoke and wrote in Latin. However, it's more than likely that original Romans, i.e., people who weren't Britons or really any other ethnic group, had either moved or outright blended with the locals.

The question remains though—what did the Anglo-Saxons do in sub-Roman Britain?

Bede attests, using a variety of sources (both oral and written, neither of which are 100% reliable) that each migration of the Angles, Saxons, and Jutes took part in three stages. The first stage would include individual mercenaries dropping by and "exploring" British soil. The next stage was migration where hundreds of tribesmen would board ships and settle in Britain, usually resulting in clashes with the locals. The final stage was establishing autonomous lands. A few less than reputable sources claim that around 441 CE most British provinces were under direct rule by the Saxons. And while there is at least some archeological evidence of burials of Angles and Saxons taking place at this period, nothing substantial can confirm that they were the overlords of the southern part of Britain during this time. Gildas does claim in his work that the East was given to the Saxons as part of a treaty the locals signed that helped alleviate some attacks by the Picts and the Scoti. The Saxons (or rather, Angles and Saxons, since Gildas used one term for these tribes) would pay tribute to the locals as a consequence of losing the Battle of Badon at some point in either the 5th or 6th century.

Eagle-eyed readers will spot that none of these dates are particularly accurate or definite. That's because sub-Roman Britain has precious little evidence to offer us. The best thing we can do is have educated guesses based on archeological, written, and oral evidence.

Chapter 2 – Early Anglo-Saxons: Origins and Pre-Settlement History

The term "Anglo-Saxon" is more modern and is a compound word defining the Germanic peoples who inhabited the isle of Britain in the early 5th century. The Anglo-Saxons themselves most certainly didn't call themselves that. Even Bede calls them by different names in different sections of his *Ecclesiastical History*.

Knowing this, it's a bit more complicated to talk about the customs and the everyday life of this people group before they settled Britain. Even the simple division of Angles and Saxons is problematic since Bede also mentions Jutes. On top of that, it's highly probable that other Germanic tribes, far smaller than these three people groups, had also raided the island during its late Roman and sub-Roman period. Batavians, for example, were used by the Roman army under Aulus Plautius to defeat the local Britons as early as 43 CE at the Battle of the Medway during the early Roman invasion of the island. Frisians were also used during this time period as mercenary fighters and made up some of the Roman cavalries as Britain was being invaded. Franks would also occasionally raid the island. The Frankish connection would actually play important political roles during the reigns of a few early Anglo-Saxon kings since their royal houses maintained close ties with the Frankish lords in mainland Europe.

The best way to approach the topic of Anglo-Saxon pre-British history is to address what we know of the three biggest tribes that Bede mentions in his *Ecclesiastical History*. To start off, we have the Angles. According to written and archeological evidence, Angles come from an area called Anglia, a small peninsula in the German federal state of Schleswig-Holstein. Anglia is actually a part of the much larger Jutland peninsula, most of which make up modern-day Denmark. Several written sources mention that Angles inhabited these lands; other than Bede, the chronicler Æthelweard and the West Saxon King Alfred the Great both identify this area as the land of Angles, and an old two-day account of a voyage by Ohthere of Hålogaland (which King Alfred later had access to) claims that this land was still inhabited by the ancestors of people living in the then-contemporary England.

Of course, we also have archeological evidence of the Angles living in Schleswig-Holstein prior to the invasion of Britain. Thorsberg moor, a peat bog on the peninsula, and Nydam Mose in Denmark both yielded a wealth of artifacts including clothes, arms, weaponry, and agricultural tools. There was also a cremation cemetery in Borgstedt, also located in Schleswig-Holstein, where archeologists unearthed urns and brooches that match those found in early 5th-century Britain. With all of this in mind, it's safe to say that we have the homeland of Angles pinned, and it's located in today's northern Germany.

When it comes to Saxons, it's important to note that their continental history continued independently centuries after some of their tribesmen settled in Britain and began forming kingdoms. The Saxons originated from Old Saxony, supposedly between the rivers Elbe, Eider, and Ems. Saxons themselves were mentioned in historical records as early as the 1st century CE. Roman historian Tacitus lists a number of different tribes, including the Angles, that all worship the same goddess. These tribes were the precursors of the

Saxons and must have already been inhabitants of Old Saxony for a period of time when Tacitus wrote about them. Greco-Roman geographer Ptolemy also seems to mention Saxons in his 2nd-century work *Geographia*, although some historians dispute this. Whatever the case may be, by the last century of Western Roman rule, the Saxons were already a well-established group of smaller pagan tribes that were raiding Britain.

Around 407 CE, when there was no feasible way for Romans to defend the Rhine, Saxons, alongside Angles and Jutes and other minor tribes, began to intensify their raids on the British, slowly inhabiting their lands. In fact, the Saxon raids were so frequent that the Romans built a set of coastal forts which had the common name of Litora Saxonica, or the Saxon Shore. By the year 442, the Saxons more or less dominated the majority of land once held by the Romans. However, Saxon history in mainland Europe doesn't end there, for centuries later, they would wage war against the newly-established kings. Charlemagne, for example, led a series of campaigns called the Saxon Wars from 772 to 804 CE. During the early days of Charlemagne's dealings with the Saxons, they were still pagans who refused to convert to Christianity. They would continue to defy the Franks until the last tribal chief was defeated in 804, which led to the Franks subjugating the Saxons and forcibly converting them to Christianity. After the conquest, the region was reorganized as the Duchy of Saxony, and in the following centuries, under Charlemagne's successors, the Saxons would remain largely loyal subjects. However, on occasion, they would rebel against their overlords, as was the case during the Saxon Rebellion of 1073 against the Salian dynasty king and Holy Roman Emperor Henry IV.

Jutes were the third tribe Bede mentions in his work. They originated from the Jutland peninsula, the modern-day location of Denmark and parts of north Germany. This location puts them neatly as contemporary "neighbors" to other tribes that would come to dominate Britain, the Angles and Saxons. Much like those two tribes, the Jutes migrated to Britain during the early 5th century CE.

When compared to Angles and Saxons, however, Jutes held smaller areas of land under their direct control. According to historical and archeological data, we can assume that Jutes ruled over Kent and the Isle of Wight, as well as the area that includes today's Hampshire. Excluding Kent, most Jutes simply assimilated into the more numerous Germanic tribes that surrounded them. Some authors even speculate that the West Saxon King Cædwalla committed something akin to genocide or ethnic cleansing of the Jutes around 686 on the Isle of Wight, but there isn't enough evidence to support this claim.

Bede states that all three people groups were led to Britain by the brothers Hengist and Horsa, though they are most likely legendary as there are no historical accounts of either of them. He even lists their ancestry, with one of their great-grandfathers being Odin himself. Considering that Bede was a Christian and a priest, it's highly unlikely that he would have accepted the existence of a pagan deity, so he most likely ascribed the name "Woden" to an earlier chieftain or king. According to the legend, the two brothers sailed from mainland Europe and landed on the Isle of Thanet, which was ruled by King Vortigern of the Britons. Much like the brothers, he was also probably a legendary figure rather than an actual historical king. During their stay on the isle, the brothers first served the king but then betrayed him. Horsa died fighting while Hengist took control and became the first king of Kent.

The names of these two brothers both relate to horses. "Horsa" is the more evident of the two, literally meaning "horse," whereas "Hengist" translates to "stallion." These brothers weren't the only pair to appear as founding brothers of a kingdom. Other Germanic groups and even other Indo-European cultures mention similar sibling pairs, leading many scholars to believe that the two are mythical rather than historical. Their influence is nonetheless still seen today, as many houses in Schleswig-Holstein and modern Lower Saxony (both original settlements of Anglo-Saxons) bear gables with two crossed horses' heads, typically called "Hengst und Hors" in German.

Whether the brothers actually existed or not, the Germanic tribes of Jutland and Old Saxony did settle Britain in the early 5th century after decades of raids and attacks on the local populace. Shortly after, they began to form their own countries and crown their own kings, a topic we will cover shortly. But it's worth pointing out that it's somewhat fascinating to know that Britain, a kingdom which will come to rule almost a quarter of the known world both in landmass and population size, came from such humble beginnings. The kings and queens of the UK wouldn't have been around if not for groups of pagan tribesmen who decided to migrate to an island they had once merely raided in order to avoid the collapse of a different major empire. When we take everything into account, we can see the story of early Angles, Saxons, and Jutes as a reminder that even the greatest of cultures come from humble beginnings.

Map of Anglo-Saxon migration in the 5th century, with Jutland, Anglia, and the Saxon coast[ii]

Chapter 3 – The Culture of Anglo-Saxons: Religion, Customs, Social Hierarchy, Early Christianity

Religion of the Anglo-Saxons

Angles, Saxons, and Jutes all belonged to a major Indo-European people group called the Germanic peoples. Like many early Indo-European cultures, the Germanic culture revolved around a polytheistic religion. However, different regions had different "takes" when it came to their pantheons. That's why, for example, historians and researchers still can't decide which deity was the head of the Slavic gods.

There's a reason to bring this up when we're talking about Anglo-Saxons. Before they converted into Christianity, they didn't have any written records of their everyday life. As such, most sources that we have on Anglo-Saxons come from later authors, like Bede and Stephen of Ripon who wrote the *Life of Saint Wilfrid*. However, these and other documents were written from the viewpoint of the Church. In other words, the authors didn't really deal with pagan traditions as much as Christianity itself. When we read these texts, we only find hints of pre-Christian customs, a word or two here, a line there. But nothing extensive, nothing concrete. Certainly nothing that can help us piece together what the ancestors of the English actually believed in.

There are, of course, other pieces of evidence, such as archeological remains found in old gravesites. One way we can learn of what certain ancient peoples believed is if we take a good look at how they buried their dead. In the overwhelming majority of cases, a person of higher status would get an elaborate burial. This wasn't just limited to kings and queens, however. Other minor members of the ruling classes, such as high priests and distinguished soldiers, would get buried in extravagant tombs with all of their belongings. We will cover these burial customs a little later.

Naturally, the most intriguing place to find traces of Anglo-Saxon religion lies within the language itself. Linguists and etymologists have looked at the different names of settlements for clues about their earliest history. Oftentimes, the Anglo-Saxons (as well as the native Britons before them) would name their cities after one of their deities or a particular practice they would engage in when it came to their religious customs. For example, terms like *hearh*, *leah*, and *weoh* translate, respectively, to "sanctuary," "holy grove" or holy woodland," and "idol, temple or shrine of a god." These words would be combined with the name of an existing deity, and later cultures would just adopt that name as the towns grew.

So, who were the gods of early Anglo-Saxons? Well, it's more than likely that their pantheon was similar, if not outright the same, as that of other Germanic tribes such as Scandinavians. There are even similarities in the names of these gods. For example, the god whose name the medieval authors mention most often in relation to old Anglo-Saxons is Woden. We can assume that he was the chief deity of the Anglo-Saxon pantheon considering how many later kingdoms claim him as their ancestor. Kings of Kent, Wessex, Mercia, and East Anglia all believed that they stemmed from Woden. If we compare his name to other Germanic gods, it's no surprise that the majority of etymologists and experts on ancient religion associate him with Odin. If Woden really is just a different pronunciation of the titular Norse god, we can assume that he was in charge of wisdom, death, healing, and other duties commonly attributed to Odin. Several towns in Britain bear Woden's name in them. These include Wenslow, Wensley, Woodnesborough, and Wansdyke. Wensley, in particular, combines Woden's name with the term *leah*, meaning that early Wensley was "Woden's holy woods." Woden was also known as Grim at this time, so places like Grimsbury, Grim's Hill, and Grim's Dyke also reference this god

Other deities also appear frequently in British place names. Tiw or Tiu (a possible equivalent of Tyr) is a god whose name we can see in Tuesley, Tysoe, and Tyesmere. Then there's Thunor (whose Norse counterpart might be Thor), and places like Thundersfield, Thunderley, and Thundersley bear his name. Considering that a few of these places have the term "holy woodland" in them, it's safe to say that these were the spots where Anglo-Saxons worshiped these particular gods. Of course, there's also the goddess Frigg. Right now, we have found little concrete evidence of Anglo-Saxons worshiping her directly in Britain, but some scholars suggest that towns such as Frobury, Freefolk, Froyle, and Frethern all contain her name.

Other minor deities could have also made up the pantheon of Anglo-Saxons. Gods like Seaxneat, Ingui, and Geat, as well as goddesses Eostre and Hretha, appear in several written sources in early Christian Anglo-Saxon literature. But there are even earlier sources. If we were to look at continental Saxons, Tacitus' work *Germania* mentions that they, alongside other Germanic tribes, worship the Earth Mother whom they call Nerthus. While there is no direct evidence that Saxons continued this practice when they migrated to Britain, it's possible that her worship survived in a different form.

Probably the most famous example of gods' names being used in everyday Anglo-Saxon speech comes from naming the days of the week. These names survive today and are well in use despite massive changes that occurred throughout the centuries of the history of Britain. In fact, this practice came from the Roman day-naming system, but nearly all of the Roman gods were replaced with their Germanic equivalents. Monday translates to "moon's day" and references the god Mani. Tuesday is obviously reserved for Tiu or Tyr. Wednesday is the most obvious here, referring to Woden. Then there's Thursday, reserved for Thunor or Thor. Friday references the goddess Frigg, while Sunday, or "sun's day," is dedicated to the goddess Sol. The only weekday that didn't get an Anglo-Saxon/Norse equivalent is Saturday, which translates to "Saturn's day." Obviously, Saturn is a Roman god, and had the Anglo-Saxons wanted to replace his name with their own divine equivalent, they'd have probably chosen Ymir.

Anglo-Saxon religion also might have included lesser fantastic beings, such as elves, dragons, and dwarves. A few old settlements contain words such as *thrys* or *draca* which mean "giants" and "dragon," hinting that the Anglo-Saxons believed in them. Other terms include *puca* (demon or goblin), *scinna* (specter or ghost), *hægtesse* (witch), and *skratti* (demon, warlock). But there is one key aspect we have to keep in mind here. Starting with 793 CE, Viking incursions in Britain became frequent. Therefore, it's safe to say that some of these names might have come from the Viking invaders settling on the isle. Both Anglo-Saxons and Vikings are Germanic in origin, so it's not out of the ordinary that they had similar beliefs and used more or less similar terminology. But even if we take the Vikings out of the equation, Anglo-Saxon place names could have come about even after they converted to Christianity.

Excavation of the Sutton Hoo burial ship, 1939[iii]

Anglo-Saxon Customs

As stated earlier, we know little of early Anglo-Saxon gods, and most of what we know from their contemporary sources was second-hand information. As such, it's difficult to talk about the customs local Anglo-Saxon people partook in with any level of certainty. However, archeological remains and even linguistic clues do provide us with a few potential scraps of information.

By far, the most direct evidence of Anglo-Saxon customs lies in how they performed their burials. Throughout the years, archeologists have unearthed many gravesites dated all the way back to the 5th century. Some of these sites include the Prittlewell royal tomb, Sutton Hoo, the Spong Hill cemetery site, Fordcroft, and Buckland. Each of these sites offers researchers a wealth of artifacts which hint at the status of the buried individuals, their potential religious beliefs, their sex, and sometimes even the cause of death.

At Spong Hill, we can find 2,316 different burials, of which only 57 so far were found to be inhumations. The rest were all cremations, whose sheer number may suggest that several towns used this area for burials. The practice of cremation is usually linked to pre-Christian cultures, considering that the Church didn't allow this practice in those times. Knowing that, we can safely assume that early Anglo-Saxons, prior to conversion, had the habit of cremating their loved ones when they passed.

But inhumations aren't exactly a custom that only Christians did. In fact, early pagan societies also had the habit of burying their dead without burning the bodies. Knowing this further complicates dating graves at gravesites like the ones at Spong Hill. After all, Angles and Saxons might have had different burial customs separately before migrating to the island.

Luckily, there is a way to distinguish Christian inhumations from pagan ones. As England became more and more Christian, rulers and priests got more modest funerals. This is not the case with pagan rulers, and we don't have to look at Anglo-Saxons to know this fact. Even early Sumerians buried their dead with a wealth of material goods, as did Egyptians and even early European societies. While there are differences regarding their methods and the amount of material that was buried with the body, generally speaking, these cultures believed that the person being buried took the objects with them to the afterlife. Anglo-Saxons surely held the same standard. In other words, a warrior being buried might need swords, daggers, shields, and armor in the afterlife, but he might also need gold, food, and decent clothing. Sometimes the burial would be somewhat extravagant, such as the case of the nobleman buried with his horse at Sutton Hoo. In Essex, a child's grave was exhumed, and it had a dog buried next to it, suggesting that the animal was the pet of the child. Other times they would get very extravagant indeed, and again, we look to Sutton Hoo for this. Namely, in 1939, archeologists unearthed an entire ship at the site. That ship contained an enormous number of items, some of which were elaborately crafted like the shoulder pads, a purse-lid, a golden buckle, and the famous Sutton Hoo helmet. Obviously, the person buried here had to be of the highest status in contemporary British society, most likely a king. Historians believe it to be Rædwald of East Anglia who ruled that same kingdom from c. 599 to c. 624 CE. While the burial itself has definite pagan elements to it, Rædwald converted to Christianity in the early years of his reign. Of course, if this burial site really is his and he really did convert to Christianity, that raises further questions regarding the wealth and the nature of the tomb.

Unfortunately, we can't tell much about the burials of common folk from these findings. However, we can assume which gender roles men and women had at the time. For example, most male graves that were exhumed contained knives and spears. These finds suggest that men were expected to be hunters, farmers, or warriors. Anglo-Saxon women were usually buried with sewing items and weaving tools, meaning they were in charge of making clothes. It should be noted that both genders had examples of elaborate, wealthy funerals, which is why some scholars speculate that early women also held power to some extent.

So, that's what we have when it comes to burials. But what about actual religious practices of the Anglo-Saxons? Is there any way we can know how they performed their rituals, how they worshiped their gods, and how this played into their everyday life?

Sadly, the best evidence we've got of this again relies on second-hand written information and early toponyms. We say "sadly" because, while these bits of evidence can be a good source of information, we still need concrete examples of Anglo-Saxon worship and customs. If we don't have these, all we have are educated guesses. So, let's delve into guessing.

Several place names in Britain suggest animal sacrifices. Gateshead and Worm's Heath are two such locations, with their original names meaning "goat's head" and "snake's head" in Old English. We even have written records of animal sacrifices occurring in the early English kingdoms, although kings began to outlaw the practice in the 7th century. There were even locations where animal carcasses were found buried alongside groups of human bodies. Most of them were oxen, but a few heads of pigs and boars were also unearthed. Sadly, we can't say for certain if these animals were buried during a sacrificial ritual or if the Anglo-Saxons simply buried fresh meat with the body of the deceased as food for the afterlife.

While animal sacrifices might have happened back then, human sacrifices in Anglo-Saxon times is still a topic open for debate. There is just no clear evidence of the ritualistic killing of humans. What we do have are 23 Sutton Hoo corpses that seem to form a circle around an area where a tree used to stand, as well as the corpse of a woman at Sewerby who might have been buried alive with her husband. Both of these claims are contested by scientists and historians, so it's hard to say if they truly represent human sacrifice or not.

Much like everything else about their customs, we barely know anything of pagan Anglo-Saxon priests. Bede mentions them in passing, and archeology hasn't yielded anything conclusive. There were corpses that were identified as male but who wore elaborate female-looking outfits which would suggest priesthood. We do know that the people believed in witches and magic considering that the Christian ruling class tried to outlaw them in the 9th century.

If Anglo-Saxon penitential, i.e., church rules and regulations, from c. 680 are to be believed, priests had issues with locals still venerating sacred trees and pillars. However, within the writings of the priest Aldhelm from this period, we don't get a clear reference to these pillars. He does call them "crude pillars," but he also mentions that they have heads of stags and snakes on the top. Certain scholars believe that Aldhelm wasn't talking about actual totem-like pillars (or menhirs) but rather real animal heads on top of spikes. Either of these fit well with Germanic customs from continental Europe, so they wouldn't really be out of place in Anglo-Saxon England, even as late as the end of the 7th century. One detail does stand out from Aldhelm's description of these practices, however. Namely, he praises the fact that most of these sites that were sacred to the pagans still living in Britain were turned into Christian holy sites, like churches. The reason this is interesting information for us is that if the Anglo-Saxons worshiped their gods by venerating tall trees or even tall wooden poles, it would be very easy to convert these spots into Christian sites. In the case of trees, all church officials would need to do is establish a new church building right next to it. When it comes to the massive poles, an additional horizontal pole would be enough to make them into crosses.

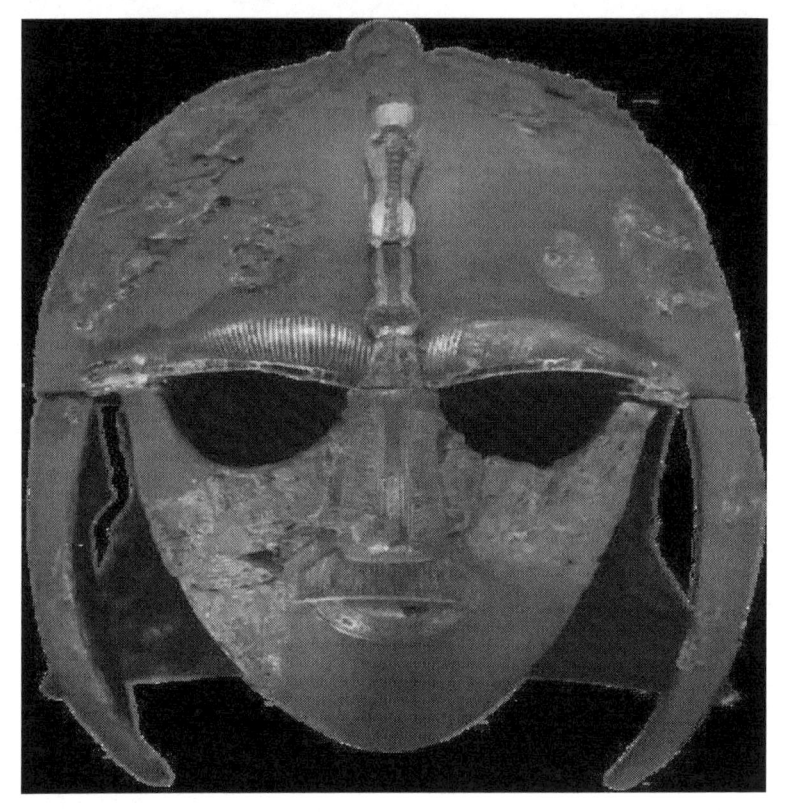

The Sutton Hoo helmet (1971 reconstruction)[iv]

Social Structure of the Anglo-Saxons

Like most European tribal cultures, the Anglo-Saxons had their own form of social stratification. Their leaders were tribal chieftains who would later bear the title of "king" (the very title "king" comes from Old English *cyning*, meaning "chieftain"). They had hereditary rights along the male line, but they didn't hold all the power, which we will get to shortly. The king was more than just a ruler, though. He was also the head judge, possibly the high priest, and a military commander, what we today would call a "commander-in-chief." Of course, we have to stress the "he" because until Mary I Tudor (known to history as Bloody Mary) came to power, no women were officially ruling over any of the Anglo-Saxon kingdoms. The king would most often rule until his death, after which a council of elders and high-ranking noblemen, the witena gemōt, would choose a new king from the royal family. Usually, the title would go to the oldest living son of the last king, and bastard children could hold no title unless they were legitimized somehow. Of course, it would be a bastard, William the Conqueror, who would take control of all of Britain in the mid-11th century, but that's a topic in and of itself that deserves a whole book.

The reason the term "king" stayed as the official title is because of its root, *cynn*. Cynn means "family, lineage," but the best term to describe it is actually the modern word that came from it, "kin." The Anglo-Saxons practiced sacral kingship, where a certain family would represent the gods (later the Christian God) on earth. This ties in well with a lot of these houses claiming kinship with the supreme god Woden. With that in mind, we can see the Anglo-Saxon king as the religious figurehead, although this role might have slightly changed with the conversion to Christianity.

The king was at the top, but the Anglo-Saxon society had a long list of titles for its other members. One title, directly under the king, was Ætheling. Æthelings were usually young princes who were heirs apparent to the throne. However, historians believe that the title might have simply been used to distinguish any young member of high nobility before the kings became more powerful on the isle, after which it became a term specific to the royal families. Æthelings are also mentioned in works of fiction such as *Beowulf*, in its very first lines no less. According to an old document most likely dating from the 900s, if you were to kill an Ætheling or harm him in any way, you'd have to pay a *weregild* or "man price" of 15,000 thrymsas (Anglo-Saxon medieval currency) or 11,250 shillings.

Each man had a weregild, i.e., his worth in gold which had to be paid as compensation if a crime was committed toward them. For comparison, a typical archbishop cost as much as an Ætheling when it came to the weregild, whereas damage to the king himself was twice that amount.

So, Æthelings were an interesting class, for sure, though we can't be sure if they held any political power while their father, the king, was still alive and ruling. Some historians state that the Anglo-Saxon kings might have ruled not as monarchs but as diarchs. In other words, a single kingdom might have been ruled over by two kings, and it would make sense that one of those two would be the heir apparent and kin to the main ruler. For this reason, Æthelings were venerated as highly as any king would.

But Æthelings were also venerated in literature and poetry. When we read early Anglo-Saxon poems, we see the term Ætheling to describe good men of noble, pure hearts. Both Beowulf and Jesus Christ are described as Æthelings a few times in medieval writing. With time, however, the title was discontinued, with some forms of the term surviving in Wales as "edling," which merely described a male heir apparent to a household.

Ealdorman was a title that meant different things at different points in time. Most people would see this term and think "Hey, these are the earliest of earls, right?" with no pun intended, of course. And they would be right. The title of earl more than likely did evolve from ealdorman, but we still have a similar-sounding title today— alderman, someone who serves on a city council. Ealdormen were actually far more influential back in the day. Namely, a typical ealdorman would be a member of the royal family or otherwise high nobility. Before the 8th century, they acted more or less independently from the king. However, in later years, ealdormen would represent former kings of territories which greater powers took under their control. In either of these positions, the ealdormen wielded great power. They presided over taxation and local courts as well as led their men into battle if there was a need for war. Any member of the ealdorman class was well respected in the community, especially if they were of a former royal bloodline. In time, these men took control of vast swathes of land, some so big they would encompass the entirety of old kingdoms. As the courts became more centralized and England moved closer to a united kingdom, ealdormen from the south would begin to attend court meetings. Historians can't be sure if ealdormen from the north were as active in attending, however. All in all, this was the highest class after the king and his direct heir.

Directly below the ealdormen were the high-reeves. Historians often associate this term to the old settlement of Bamburgh where they would often use the term "high-reeve" for its own magnates and independent lords. However, there's evidence of other members of lower nobility throughout Anglo-Saxon England bearing this title. High-reeves had to respond directly to an ealdorman, but they could still lead local, provincial armies independently.

Reeves were one class below high-reeves, and they would directly oversee a manor, a town, a district, or anything of a similar size. Before we get into what a reeve was responsible for, we should mention how land was structured in early medieval England. Namely, if you had arable land for one household, you had a *hide*. Ten hides would make up a *tything*, while ten tythings formed a *hundred*. But it didn't even end there. If you were to group several hundreds, you'd get an administrative unit called the *shire*. The term itself is often used in place names, such as Berkshire, Cheshire, Worcestershire, Yorkshire, and so on.

With all of this in mind, we can see that different units of land demanded different types of reeves. The list included shire-reeves (the origin of today's sheriff), town-reeves, port-reeves, reeves of hundreds, and reeves of manors. A typical reeve had the duty of a local policeman, job overseer, and manager. In short, he had to take care of the territory he was assigned to for his lords.

The next class was the thegns. A thegn was, in the beginning, a term used for military servicemen loyal to the king. It gradually shifted into representing members of the lower class who would work on different units of land, such as hundreds. They were directly under the ealdormen and reeves, but at times, a king could choose his own personal thegn whom only he could depose. In addition, this king's thegn only took orders from the monarch directly.

All of these titles were the titles of free men, and the lowest of these is the ceorl, also known as churl. This very term gave us the names Charles and Carl. Churls could cultivate land without a lot of restrictions, and their loyalty was to the king. To put it simply, they were free to farm and live their lives, unlike the classes below them. During the reign of Anglo-Saxon kingdoms, the churls didn't have a lot of legal trouble with their land ownership. However, with the conquest of William the Conqueror, this class slowly began to erode. At some point, the term "churl" began to be used as a pejorative toward the lower classes in general. However, its original meaning had nothing to do with class; it simply meant "man" or "husband."

Cotters were similar to churls, but unlike churls, they couldn't really own land. They had to rent arable land from local lords, which made them directly subservient to them. In later years, after the Conquest, the cotters would work under a new class called the villeins, but different accounts lump these two classes into one because of how similar they were.

Last on the list were slaves. Officially, slavery was abolished in the UK in 1833 with the Slavery Abolition Act. However, even during the Anglo-Saxon period, people would sentence slave traders to pay the weregild of the man they sold. It didn't matter if this man committed any crime; the seller still had to pay the penalty. Slaves as a class in Britain at the time had no civil liberties. Before the kingdoms were established on the island, the Anglo-Saxon tribes would capture local Britons and use them for slave labor. Wars were also good opportunities to snatch a new batch of slaves, and families could even sell their own children into slavery to pay outstanding debts. This entire practice is not dissimilar from slavery during ancient Mesopotamian kingdoms and empires. Kinsmen of slaves could even buy the freedom of their captive relatives, and if a person were to become a slave due to debt, they could work it off in several years and earn their own freedom back.

There is evidence of slave trades going on even after 1066. Despite the taxation and legal penalties, the Anglo-Saxons still occasionally sold slaves to other kingdoms on the continent.

Early Christianity

It took a fair while to Christianize the Anglo-Saxon kingdoms. Not only was the pagan religion still strong, but even after the first Christian kings began the process of conversion, there were monarchs and subjects who would go back to their old ways. It was a difficult process, and it all started in 597 in Kent.

The first Anglo-Saxon ruler to convert to Christianity was King Æthelberht of Kent. His own wife, Bertha, was of Merovingian nobility and Christian herself, and he allowed her to restore an old Roman church and to worship Christ. The church she restored is the famed Church of St. Martin in Canterbury. Sometime after this event, Æthelberht wrote to Pope Gregory I in Rome and asked him to send over missionaries to begin converting the Kentish. This was done by a man who would become the first Archbishop of Canterbury called Augustine in 597 when he landed on the isle of Thanet in the spring. Though he wasn't initially too enthusiastic about this mission, Augustine still managed, with Æthelberht's approval, to convert 10,000 of the king's subjects by Christmas. That's 10,000 people in less than nine months!

By 601, Augustine had been trying to expand his mission to other cities. He appointed two bishops, Mellitus and Justus, in London and Rochester respectively, but failed to convert most of the men his mission entailed. He died in 604 before he could see his new monastery, the Church of St. Peter and Paul, finished and operational. He was buried there and later venerated as St. Augustine of Canterbury, the first Archbishop of Canterbury and the "apostle to the English." A little over a decade later, King Æthelberht died as well, leaving Kent in religious "ruins" as heathens and pagans began to reclaim authority.

Years later, in 664, the Northumbrian King Oswiu, alongside the Bishop St. Wilfrid, decided to follow the laws of the Roman Church and renounce the Celtic practices. According to their decision, discussed and accepted during the Synod of Whitby, the Church was to answer only to the archbishop and the pope in Rome, not to the local monarchs. In addition, the Canterbury archbishops would, from that point forward, receive their palliums from the pope, and this tradition would remain more or less the same until the Reformation.

Christianity was still very young even two centuries after Æthelberht's bold move and Oswiu's decision at Whitby. However, the Anglo-Saxon missionaries were already wandering the continent in order to convert the Frankish to Christianity. St. Boniface was an instrumental figure in this movement, and he began to urge for conversions of continental Saxons as early as the late 7th century. Even during the last three decades of the 8th century, when Charlemagne was ruling over vast swathes of Central Europe, the Anglo-Saxon missionaries were converting the local populace. Their missions were instrumental in Christianizing the newly-formed Germanic states, and every subsequent mission to other areas of Europe came from the Holy Roman Empire.

On the one hand, it's a bit disappointing how little we know of actual pagan customs from the times of early Anglo-Saxons. It's additionally frustrating when we learn that a lot of their sacred places were either converted to churches or just outright leveled. Place names and archeological remains can only take us so far, but in order to understand how early Anglo-Saxon pagans operated, we need more information. On the other hand, though, it's interesting how turbulent early English Christianity really was. There's really something fascinating about kingdoms basically waging war over who will convert or not in the early 7th century and then suddenly sending effective and successful missions to Central Europe mere decades later. It's truly amazing to see how a new religion spread so fast in such a small area and then to influence an entire continent by means of conversion.

Chapter 4 – Everyday Life of Anglo-Saxon England: Jobs and Division of Labor, Food and Drink, Clothes, Architecture, Travel, Wars, Gender and Age Norms, Art, Written Works

Jobs and Division of Labor

Anglo-Saxons may have started their interaction with Britain as raiders and warriors, but as they continued to settle the island, their lifestyle didn't differ too much from any other early medieval community. Of course, it goes without saying that Angles, Saxons, and Jutes weren't sailors and raiders when they were still in continental Europe. They had to produce and provide food for their families, create and repair weapons and armor, make clothing and shoes, spread the word of God to the laity, trade goods, build houses, and maintain order within their community.

We've already discussed the social hierarchy of early Anglo-Saxons, from kings to slaves, so we can see from these classes themselves what some social duties of both the nobles and the common folk were. Very broadly speaking, the ealdormen had political and judicial power. They would elect the new king from his family, pass laws, judge potential criminals, call for wars, and enforce the laws. They didn't have as much of a hands-on approach to the people as did local reeves, who were responsible for both the land they held and the people working or living on it. In other words, the nobles were responsible for the law.

It's also evident from both pagan and Christian Anglo-Saxon kingdoms that priests had privileges. After all, they were responsible for the spiritual support of the local community. If we take all the evidence about the pagan kingdoms as true (despite the massive speculation we already noted in earlier chapters), we can assume that rituals were an important part of "staying alive." In November, according to a collection of works known as Old English Martyrology, the priests had to sacrifice a lot of cattle to their gods. Usually, these sacrifices were to appease the gods so that they could, in turn, give the people agreeable climate conditions and not have them starve or die of a plague. With Christian priests, the privileges were even greater but so were the responsibilities. Even with Augustine's arrival in 597 and his subsequent work, the vast majority of the country was pagan, and they all needed conversion. Considering that travel back then was done on foot or on horseback, and that most pagan kings fully opposed converting to Christianity and had armies to back them up if any Christians wanted to convert them by force, Augustine's conversion of 10,000 Kentish people in a matter of months really deserves a decent level of respect.

So those are the nobles and the priests, and their work was pretty simple—one group was to maintain law, the other to provide religious support and spread the word of God. But there were other jobs in Anglo-Saxon England largely performed by the poorest members of society, either churls or slaves.

The most common occupation was that of a farmer. Farmers would normally be men, and they would tend to their field, the aforementioned hide. At this point in history, plows had developed to cut deeper into the ground which yielded better crops. It was, of course, common to use beasts of burden for this task. But even with the help of animals and with better plows, farm work was still incredibly hard.

But food didn't just come from farming. Other men would often go hunting, and it wasn't that uncommon to take your ten-year-old son with you. Fishing was another way to get food, especially by the seaside. However, the most effective way of getting meat was to herd animals. Anglo-Saxons favored beef, but they herded more than just cattle. They also took care of sheep, goats, and pigs. Poultry was also raised, and people kept flocks of chickens, geese, ducks, herons, plovers, and grouses. Most of these jobs were performed by men; however, we will look at women in Anglo-Saxon communities in just a little bit.

Metalworking was already a common practice throughout Europe, and Anglo-Saxon smiths were exceptional. From the numerous mounds and gravesites, archeologists have found a wealth of different weapons and tools made of iron. These include swords, daggers, shields, knives, axes, pickaxes, shovels, hammers, and other tools. Woodworking was also widespread as tools were uncovered that the medieval people used to shape and cut wood. Many needles and spindle parts were also found, so we can safely conclude that Anglo-Saxon people, in particular women, were skilled seamstresses.

Potters also had a lot of work on their hands considering the wealth of pots, bowls, urns, and other "dishes" found in Anglo-Saxon graves. Some of these creations were very elaborate, suggesting that they were used by royal families. And speaking of elaborate, plenty of brooches, ornaments, and beads were found that were expertly worked on, suggesting that Anglo-Saxon jewelers had perfected the craft quite well.

In terms of making food and drink, both men and women did their fair share of the work. Women made cheese, brewed alcohol, baked bread, and milked cows, but it was the men who did the actual cooking. Linguistic evidence suggests that no female cooks existed in early Anglo-Saxon England, but that they were able to bake bread.

But baking bread wasn't the only occupation where you'd see both Anglo-Saxon men and women. "Breaking bread," i.e., attending feasts, also included both genders. Typically, women would serve men their drinks at feasts, and a feast could be organized by either the king himself or even one of the thegns for his local community. That way, any woman, from queen to commoner, had the duty to serve drinks, though the task typically fell on lower-class women if they were attending. In addition, both men and women could perform as traveling actors, musicians, singers, and entertainers. The Anglo-Saxons led a hard life with lots of violence, hard work, and constant threats of death, but they also played hard, with lots of drinks, dancing, singing, and having a good time overall.

Food and Drink

As stated, Anglo-Saxons had several different ways of producing food for their community. In terms of meat, they had hunting and herding, largely of cattle and sheep. However, it's interesting to note that only pigs were solely raised to be eaten. Nearly every other animal that would be herded had more than one purpose. For example, an Anglo-Saxon would herd sheep for meat but also for their wool. Cattle produced milk if they were cows or were used to plow the land if they were bulls. Both cows and bulls would provide hides as well as meat when they were slaughtered, but interestingly enough, they would also use connective tissue of cows to make primitive glue. This wasn't really an exclusively Anglo-Saxon practice as even ancient Egypt used to make glue from different animals. Cow horns were also used to make drinking cups. One more useful animal part the Anglo-Saxons often used was the fat, and they used it to make oils for oil lamps. And no, poultry wasn't excluded from this either. Hollow chicken bones were, for example, used to make musical pipes. Even wild game wasn't just hunted for the meat. Deer would provide the Anglo-Saxon hunter with antlers and skins, while the tusks of hunted wild boars presented some of the greatest trophies at the time.

The Anglo-Saxons were avid farmers, and they grew a wide range of different crops. These ranged from rye and wheat to barley. Each of these was later used to make bread and/or beer. But the Anglo-Saxons also grew vegetables, such as peas, carrots, cabbages, parsnips, and celery, as well as fruit like apples, sloes, and different types of berries.

Dairy products also played a major part in Anglo-Saxon lives, so milk, butter, and cheese were common among the early kingdoms, especially with the common folk. Noblemen were the only ones who could actually afford to eat meat frequently as it was a luxury the churls could only sometimes afford. Poultry was also frequent in Anglo-Saxon times, and while they did eat chicken and duck meat, the lower classes would mostly raise them for their eggs. A typical churl meal would include bread, cheese, and eggs, and these eggs could either come from domesticated birds such as chickens, ducks, and geese, or from wild birds. Fish-wise, the Anglo-Saxons preferred the taste of herring, eel, salmon, perch, pike, and roach. Fish remains were found in Anglo-Saxon toilet pits suggesting that they ate them frequently. In fact, a 10th-century text called Ælfric's *Colloquy* contains an interesting passage about how Anglo-Saxon people fished. From this text, we see that the medieval people of England enjoyed a wide range of both freshwater and saltwater fishes.

Breadmaking was equally as important as fishing, if not more so. Women would bake bread on a griddle or in a clay oven, while the flour would be grinded on a separate hand quern, i.e., a stone used to help grind various materials by hand. Sometimes the baker would grind the flour at a water mill nearby. Anglo-Saxon houses usually contained a central hearth, and oftentimes, there would be a cauldron there. That's where the cook prepared soups or stews that were just as common as bread among the lower Anglo-Saxon classes.

There were plenty of other food sources, such as wild birds, hares, and wild berries. And of course, you can't have a meal without having something to drink.

Surprisingly, the Anglo-Saxons didn't drink a lot of pure, clear water. The reasons for this are multiple. For instance, there were no systems of catching rainwater that could supply an entire settlement. And most of the freshwater inland was polluted or otherwise impure to drink. Lastly, sea water, at least for those settlements that were on the coast, wasn't (and still isn't) good for humans to drink because of its contents. As such, the Anglo-Saxons would use barley to make very light beer. It wasn't rich in alcohol, but it could quench the thirst of anyone, from children to adults. Stronger alcohol was also made, but the drink most Anglo-Saxons seemed to favor was mead. Mead is made from fermented honey. Since sugar wasn't available at the time, most people ate honey if they wanted to sweeten their food. In fact, most houses would have a beehive or two nearby. Drinking mead was already a major part in feasting of local chieftains, hence the term "mead-hall" which we famously know from *Beowulf*. Ealdormen, kings, and other wealthy men could sometimes indulge themselves in wine. However, very few people within the Anglo-Saxon kingdoms made wine, so they had to import it from the Mediterranean.

We already mentioned cow horns being used as cups. However, wealthy families had metal goblets for their drinks during feasts, and even their cutlery and eating utensils were elaborate. However, the churls would eat using more modest tools. For example, there were no forks at the time, so everyone used knives and wooden spoons. A churl would often eat from a simple clay or wooden bowl. There are some hints in written texts about leather drinking cups, but no evidence of these has been found by archeologists yet.

Clothes

Early Anglo-Saxons didn't use clothing to distinguish different statuses, but as both the kingdoms and the clergy developed, this class divide was beginning to show even in what they wore. For example, silk was a material that was mostly worn by the rich, specifically kings, queens, and members of the clergy. When it came to the clothing of the common folk, they largely used linen and wool.

Average men of the lowest status could only afford to wear a simple tunic. Higher status usually meant you could afford a pair of trousers and even an undertunic as well. They also wore caps and leather shoes. Women would wear gowns, and depending on their status, they would either have a simple, standard gown or an elaborate piece containing an undergown and an outer gown. Cloaks were also common with both sexes, though men wore them more frequently, and kings' cloaks had more elements to them. Kings would even have a leather tunic with sewn rings to distinguish them from the common folk.

In terms of priests, they had to wear simple clothes that didn't contain any bright, distracting colors. As the 11th century rolled by, they wore an elaborate set of clothes such as the dalmatics (a specific type of tunic), the chasuble (a priest's vestment), and different types of hats. However, these elaborate clothes were reserved for archbishops and bishops. Regular monks had rougher, simpler clothing.

Anglo-Saxon Architecture

Medieval buildings were not as diverse as they are today. We can classify them into two distinct categories: secular buildings and church buildings.

Let's start with secular buildings. However, the very term "secular" is a bit misleading since we're talking about everyday houses and great halls. Perhaps the better term would be "vernacular structures." However, the semantics of their name doesn't really matter, but their purpose does. Anglo-Saxons lived in very primitive houses. These houses came in two types, with the second, the above-ground house, later developing into a hall. The first type was the so-called "sunken-featured building" or SFB for short. Initially, archeologists simply called them "pit-houses," and at first glance, they do have an obvious feature of a pit-house, namely the pit. However, SFBs are a bit more elaborate. We also know that these were not Roman or Celtic houses since there is evidence of SFBs in modern-day Germany as well. Here, they have the common name *Grubenhäuser*, which translates to "grubhouses, grubhuts."

A typical SFB has a simple, thatched roof. Examples of wooden shingles and turf roofs also exist, but they were not that common back in the day. This simple roof would have gables as well as a hole for smoke to come out. The entire body of the house was usually made of wood with main support posts rammed deep into the ground. And then there's the pit itself. Usually it would be dug into the floor and possibly covered by a wooden floor. Some have speculated that this hole was used for storage, while others interpret the whole SFB to not be a house of a commoner but a weaving shed. Remains of looms were found at a few of these SFBs which seem to corroborate this fact. Most historians would agree that buildings like this could very well serve more than one purpose.

The interior of these houses was simple. There was just one room where a family did everything. They slept, ate, received guests, and conversed regularly there. Churls would not normally have beds, so they simply slept on floors. Even their cattle would spend the night inside of the hut, which actually helped during the winter as the extra bodies helped keep the temperature high. The houses had no windows, while the toilets were merely pits in the ground outside the home surrounded by wattle walls. What we would call a toilet seat today was nothing more than a broad plank with a hole in it during Anglo-Saxon times.

In terms of raw materials, above-ground houses were not much sturdier. They were usually built from wood too. The big difference (no pun intended) was the size. Above-ground houses would be far larger, usually rectangular or square. They would also have a thatched roof with a hole in it, but unlike SFBs, these houses had windows. These early windows were merely halls in walls with no glass, and they were called "eye-holes."

These houses would eventually evolve into halls. During Anglo-Saxon times, a hall was an important building, considering it housed the local chieftain or king. Much like SFBs, halls had a single large room with a hearth in the middle. However, the sheer size of the hall gave it more features. For example, an entire wall could have been dedicated to keeping the cattle in for the winter. In addition, the walls were larger and taller so Anglo-Saxon chieftains would decorate them with various trophies. Deer antlers were a popular choice, as we saw in the food and drink section earlier. The halls would also feature shields and spears mounted onto them.

Halls had a great significance for the local populace. The king would summon his subjects for feasts and celebrations after a war or during a festival. Women would pour mead or strong beer while game was roasted on an open fire in the middle. After the meal was done, minstrels would sing songs of heroism, war, hunting, and everyday life. Halls were also places where chieftains planned battles, settled disputes, and generally performed their civic duties. Other times they would just use them as any other house.

However, even the halls weren't perfect. Their floors would often be dirty and uneven, despite evidence that some of these halls had wooden floors. Because of how open these halls were, they weren't immune to the smell or the noise from outside. In other words, despite its high status in early Anglo-Saxon society, the hall was still not the prettiest place to live and was little more than an average house.

Archeologists still don't know a lot about these early Anglo-Saxon dwellings; however, there are places that provide us with enough detail for a basic idea. West Stow, for example, is an open-air museum where we have archeological remains of houses dating back to the Mesolithic era. A huge section of this site is reserved for early Anglo-Saxon dwellings which have been reconstructed and can be visited today. There were no less than seven potential halls uncovered at this area, as well as various SFBs, potential animal dens, and other unidentified buildings.

As stated, most of these dwellings were made of wood, so it's difficult to find any actual physical remains of these houses. However, early Anglo-Saxons did use stone for other types of buildings, and more often than not, they were churches.

As we saw, the earliest surviving church from the Anglo-Saxon period is the St. Martin's Church in Canterbury. Before it was rebuilt by Augustine, it was a private chapel used by Queen Bertha of Kent. Augustine did major reconstruction on the church but wouldn't live to see it finished. Of course, it's far from being the only church from this period.

Looking at St Martin's Church and other contemporary buildings, we can spot a few key elements to how they were built. For instance, the quoins, or cornerstones, were usually arranged in a long-and-short pattern. To elaborate, the pattern consisted of alternating horizontal and vertical stones. The Minster Church of St. Mary is the perfect example of how these stones look in practice. In fact, these slim vertical stones are called "pilaster strips" and are one of the most common features of Anglo-Saxon church architecture.

Most of these churches would have double-triangular windows on the western walls of the nave, which is the central part of the church. Other church windows would be narrow and have round arches, and most of the time, when masons built these arches, they simply reused Roman stones during construction. Their walls were made using herringbone stonework, and they had a narthex, or a west porch opposite the main altar. We should note that churches of this era rarely had more than one of the features listed here.

Northern churches had more of a Celtic design to them, being very narrow with no aisles and a rectangular chancel, a part near the altar separated from the nave by either a screen or stairs. On the other hand, each of the southern churches from this period, like the ones at Kent, was small and had a simple layout based on Roman basilicas, i.e., they had rounded chancels in the east of the building and plain-looking walls. Only with the Norman invasion would the rulers begin to rebuild the churches, making them more elaborate and grander in size and scale.

One interesting detail about northern Anglo-Saxon church architecture, in particular, was the stone crosses. Many of these crosses would be found at crossroads in places like Dearham, Bakewell, Bewcastle, Gosforth, Ilkley, and Irton. Like the surviving churches of the north from that period, these large stone crosses had Celtic designs, which suggests an influence of the local Britons on the settling Anglo-Saxons. The crosses weren't a part of any building but were built next to public road intersections and other roadside areas. If we take into account that the early Anglo-Saxons and Britons were pagans who worshiped their gods by venerating massive pillars and trees, this could easily explain why these crosses wound up there in the first place. Even Pope Gregory I urged Augustine to simply "repurpose" old religious sites into Christian churches and places of prayer. Church officials could have easily replaced these pillars with stone crosses since the place itself already had a heavy religious significance to the local pagans. At times, even entire churches were built right next to or even around these crosses.

Of course, there were even a few "secular buildings" made of stone that weren't churches. For example, local Anglo-Saxons didn't want to live in old Roman settlements, opting to build their own houses closer to arable farmland or rivers plentiful with fish. The more these settlements grew, the bigger their need was to have some sort of protection. As such, they would construct stone fortifications to defend themselves against invading Vikings. These fortifications were called burhs, and sadly, none remain standing to this day. However, some archeologists suggest that St. George's Tower at

Oxford, dating back to the 11th century, was actually a part of a larger defensive structure that surrounded the local burh at the time.

The chancel wall with Roman bricks, St. Martin's Church, Canterbury[v]

Travel

By land or sea, the Anglo-Saxons moved a lot. After all, it's hard to believe that they swam across the English Channel to invade late Roman Britain. Clearly, the early Germanic tribes had some sort of ship that was capable of traversing the restless ocean.

One popular theory is that the early ships of Angles, Saxons, and Jutes had no masts. They were very long and, of course, made of wood. The fact that they were long is important since they wanted to fit as many of their soldiers onto the ship as possible. We can have some idea of what these ships looked like if we examine the reconstructed ships such as the Nydam boat, the Gredstedbro boat (both found in Denmark), and the boat used in the Sutton Hoo princely burial. All three of these ships had keel planks rather than proper keels, were over 20 meters or 65 feet long, and had no mast blocks. If we were to assume that similar boats were used to cross the Channel, we could ascertain that the Anglo-Saxons were strong, experienced naval travelers who raided Britain with simple ships, oars, and brute strength.

In addition to ships, the Anglo-Saxons also probably had smaller river frigates. Local river sailing would be common during that time, especially with the emergence of trading and the expansion of towns and cities.

Ground travel was a bit more diverse. Naturally, locals traveled either on foot or on horseback. Horses, in particular, were very significant to the Anglo-Saxons of the period. The most obvious example includes the names of the supposed ancestors of Kent, Hengist and Horsa, but other evidence also lies in place names such as Studham, Stadhampton, and Stoodleigh, each of them containing the term "stud." In regards to religious purposes, horses would be frequent motifs in certain tales of miracles with early Anglo-Saxon Christians, such as the horse who helped St. Cuthbert from starving or the horse who sank into the ground where St. Boniface died and when they pulled it out uncovered a fountain of drinking water. It's hard to overemphasize how important horses were to the ancestors of modern British people. However, they also had a lot of practical uses. For example, several different types of horses are named within Old English. There were cart horses, pack horses, riding horses, breeding horses, royal and aristocratic horses, and war horses. While it's tempting to think that they also used horses for plowing, there is no recorded evidence for this, nor is there a term for "plow horse" in Old English.

Judging by these words, we can see that the Anglo-Saxons most often used horses to transport goods. For example, a horse might drag along a cart of hay or vegetables, or an owner might place a lot of baggage onto its back. In terms of riding, Anglo-Saxon warriors were famous (or rather infamous) for being among the first people on the island to actually raid on horseback. One more purpose that these horses served was a bit unorthodox but still highly possible. Namely, in times of food shortages such as harsh winters, Anglo-Saxons would eat their horses. They would also eat them after they became too old for riding or pulling carts. However, the occurrence is only unorthodox if we understand how important horses actually were to this culture. During the later periods of Anglo-Saxon kingdoms, they founded a lot of horse-breeding establishments.

Horses were, in fact, so valuable that an Anglo-Saxon man could use one in land trade or gift one as a sign of respect or even for a dowry. Royalty, in particular, held these animals in high esteem, and as we saw in the earlier chapters, one unknown prince was actually found buried with his horse.

The methods are there—horseback, foot, boat, ship—but there's still a question of where the Anglo-Saxons traveled. Or, to be more precise, did the Anglo-Saxons use roads?

In modern Italy, you can still find old roads that the ancient Romans built. However, in pre-Anglo-Saxon England, even the Romans used roads that were built before them. Namely, there is some physical evidence of ditched roads that connected early Iron Age settlements of Kent thousands of years before Romans even set foot on British soil. Naturally, once Rome took control, the new overlords made sure to reuse and rebuild these roads, alongside a few new ones.

But the Anglo-Saxons didn't merely use the roads built by their ancestors. Excavations done at the Pilgrim's Way, which stretches from Winchester to the shrine of St. Thomas Becket at Canterbury, uncovered three separate hollow ways. They were carbon-dated to anywhere between the 7th and the 10th century, suggesting that it was the local Anglo-Saxon community that built them. Other ways of tracking these old roads include wayside markers, but they are few and far between, such as the Copplestone Cross in Devon.

Scientists have used methods such as LiDAR (Light Detection and Ranging) remote sensing and movement of objects to determine the potential old routes that the Anglo-Saxons and the Romans before them used. The findings give us a decent network of roads, some of which became obsolete near the end of the 10th century. However, it's important to note that not all Anglo-Saxon kingdoms stopped using Roman roads at the same time. It was more of a gradual change, with Mercia and East Anglia using Roman roads the longest out of all the kingdoms.

Other evidence of different roads exists within place names and textual sources. For example, Sturton Grange, a parish in Leeds, derives its name from the term "street." The name would suggest that the settlement was next to a major road. When it comes to written sources, we can look to the Anglo-Saxon charters, which were Old English documents that detailed and listed land grants and privileges of the laity. From these documents, we can look at the old descriptions of landmarks close to the boundaries of private land and determine if they have any characteristics of old Anglo-Saxon roads.

Usually, the Anglo-Saxon traveler would walk, march, or ride a horse using one of these many roads. However, straying off the path would have been dangerous. During the old kingdoms, raids and roadside robberies were common. An interesting fact to note is that the Anglo-Saxons made use of rivers as waterways far more commonly than their Roman predecessors. Even when they walked, they opted to follow the rivers as they were safer. Traveling was often painfully slow, so many people simply didn't leave their town that often.

Wars

Anglo-Saxons were a people of war well before they inhabited Britain. They were raiding the shores of Britain in the late 4th century alongside multiple other tribes, and when the 5th century rolled in, they were already settling on the island. However, a warrior culture like that of Germanic tribes doesn't become purely agricultural overnight. During their early years, the Anglo-Saxons waged quite a few wars against both foreign and domestic threats.

The earliest enemies of the Anglo-Saxons were the local Britons and their Roman rulers. With the Romans still being nominally in power, they treated the newly-settled Anglo-Saxons as they would treat any other tribe—they imposed taxes and looked upon them as barbarians. The new tribes soon began to rebel quite often. The first territory to fall under Anglo-Saxon, or rather Jutish control, was Kent. But the Britons didn't really surrender, though they were losing ground fast.

This is where the possibly mythical figure of King Arthur comes into focus. Arthur, as the legends and a few scarce written records state, beat the Saxons at the Battle of Badon, which, if true, occurred around 500 CE. It is very difficult to overemphasize how divided scientists and historians are about the historicity of this king and battle. One detail that makes the Battle of Badon more fictional than real is that Arthur allegedly killed 960 Saxon soldiers himself. This is, of course, an exaggeration, possibly for poetic purposes, because even with modern weapons, a single person cannot kill 960 people and live to tell the tale. However, one thing is for certain. Even if the Battle of Badon didn't happen and King Arthur didn't exist, the Britons did successfully push away the Saxons, but as the centuries rolled on, they lost more and more territory. By the end of the 7th century, the Britons were relegated to the area of Britain which makes up modern-day Wales today. During that time, the Anglo-Saxon kingdoms were slowly blooming and coming into power. This was clearly no longer a Britain of Celts or Romans, that much was clear.

The Celts of Wales weren't about to give up, however. Different independent kingdoms formed after 500 CE in the area, some of which include Powys, Gwynedd, Morgannwg, and Gwent. These kingdoms, especially Powys and Gwynedd, would successfully fend off the advances of the Anglo-Saxon kingdom of Mercia, which was expanding rapidly. After a series of battles, Mercian kings began to construct dykes, and stricter borders were established between the Anglo-Saxons and the surviving Britons. Soon after, during the mid-9th century, the Vikings would invade the island, and some Welsh kings, notably the king of Gwynned called Anarawd ap Rhodri, allied with the Norsemen at first in order to reclaim some lands, but soon after these alliances broke, they joined forces with King Alfred of Wessex, later known as Alfred the Great, against the invaders.

Naturally, the Vikings were a threat long before the Welsh allied with them. They began their raids of the island in the last decades of the 8th century. They first began raiding monasteries and churches since they were by far the wealthiest establishments in any kingdom, coastal or landlocked. But the Vikings didn't just stop at raids. By the 9th century, they were already settling on the island while continuing to raid local territories. They even had a large standing army, which we know from their conquest of York in 866. It would be Alfred the Great that would defeat the Vikings in 878 at the Battle of Edington. Most of the Vikings then moved to the northeastern part of the island, with the remaining territories being Anglo-Saxon.

The Vikings that raided and warred against the Anglo-Saxons were Danes, and their defeat at Edington didn't stop them from continuing to attack the locals. In 1013, the Danes conquered and ruled the island under the leadership of Sweyn Forkbeard until his death a year later. The Danes came back in 1016 and reconquered the land, and their ruler, Cnut the Great, Forkbeard's son, was crowned king of England a year later. He ruled as a king of a united Norway, Denmark, and England from 1028 until 1035 when he died. He was succeeded by his two sons, Harold Harefoot and Harthacnut, who both ruled very briefly (1035-1040 and 1040-1042). After their deaths, an Anglo-Saxon king, Edward the Confessor, took the throne and ruled until 1066.

Obviously, 1066 is a major year for the history of England. Not only was it the year when Edward the Confessor died, but it was also the year when his successor, Harold Godwinson, took the throne. Sadly, he would only maintain this position for nine months. During 1066, William the Bastard of Normandy and his troops began their conquest of England. In October of that same year, at the Battle of Hastings, Harold would die, leaving the throne open for his successor, Edgar Ætheling. Edgar was even elected to be the proper heir by the witena gemōt, but he never took the throne because of William. Edgar's own story didn't end there, however, but that's when the story of Norman Britain began and when the Anglo-Saxons officially lost control of Britain.

Naturally, the Anglo-Saxons remained the majority even after William's conquest, though the multiple people groups began to assimilate more and more in later years. It's also safe to say that wars and invasions didn't end with William. Many other people groups would attack the island, but in terms of Anglo-Saxon kingdoms and their wars, they ended in 1066.

Of course, these were just the wars against outside forces. There were a lot of battles and skirmishes between the Anglo-Saxon kingdoms themselves, a topic that will be addressed in the following chapter. Now, however, is a good time to take a look at how Anglo-Saxons conducted warfare.

Anglo-Saxon warfare changed as the centuries moved along. Their armies first consisted of small, tribal groups of warriors. As the 11th century rolled in, they already had a unified island and their armies were more organized and uniform. In terms of weapons, they used swords, javelins, spears, and missile-launching slingshots. It should be noted that a "missile" here refers to anything that can be thrown, such as an ax or an arrow, but when it comes to slingshots, it's usually a round, heavy stone. There are hints of Anglo-Saxon soldiers using archers in battles but not enough for anything conclusive.

When it came to group battles, the soldiers would form shield walls. As the name suggests, these were human walls of shields. Anglo-Saxon historian Stephen Pollington has suggested a possible sequence of events during a fight. First, the king or commander would line up the troops and provide an inspirational speech. Next, there would be a battle cry, and one or both sides would advance with the shield walls. Then, as they charged, they would hurl missiles at the opposite side to dissuade them from clashing, and once they got within range, the two shield walls would collide. One side would push forward with weapons, whereas the other would try to hold the line. If no side budged, they would retreat for a rest, hurling a few more missiles at each other in the meantime. These steps would get repeated until one side broke and the other advanced.

During these battles, individuals would separate themselves and move ahead of the group to throw their javelins. This left them exposed to the javelins of the other side, and once a thrower was killed, a soldier could cross into the land between the armies and claim his armor and weapons. These actions were considered acts of bravery, and the person who would expose themselves like this would get material awards and recognition if he survived the battle.

A few instances of using horses in battle exist but not enough to have a definite picture of horseback warfare in Anglo-Saxon kingdoms. There is also not a lot of evidence for training or army supplies, but it's safe to assume that soldiers practiced wrestling, jumping, running, and throwing spears. These would help them get ready for battle and keep them in shape.

Abingdon sword, c. 9th century, found at Abingdon, Oxfordshire[vi]

Gender and Age Norms

Medieval societies like Anglo-Saxon kingdoms were patriarchal in nature. That means the men would hold political power and be heads of religious institutions. They would also be the majority of landowners and would go to war. Modern gender theories usually reject medieval societies as regressive in terms of treatment of women, but in reality, the Anglo-Saxon society was less clear-cut than that. In other words, women had their fair share of positive and negative aspects in early Britain.

When it came to the Church, women gained a lot of new opportunities with the introduction of Christianity. England was one of the first countries to begin venerating women as saints after their passing, for example. Not to mention that there were separate monasteries for men and women back then, allowing women to become abbesses. With this position, she could handle the finances of local communities as well as the property of the church. Usually, it would be women of noble birth that would take monastic vows and become abbesses, making them heads of different churches. Considering how important the Church was as an institution back then, this was a major shift in how women normally behaved or were treated in Anglo-Saxon communities. Of course, they would still be appointed to these positions by men, and the archbishops themselves were still male.

Women who were nuns and abbesses were greatly respected and admired by the local communities of laymen. They were seen as paragons of virtue and chastity, having renounced their bodily desires and joined the clergy. This made them no less respected than the men in those same positions, as joining the church was generally seen as a noble and pure act.

In terms of queens and noble women, we know from written sources and even some literary works, like *Beowulf*, that they had the task of serving drinks during feasts at grand halls. Of course, a queen didn't have to serve drinks if there were women of lower stature present. Women would also not participate in battle, and written records of any women taking up arms are scarce. They would also not do any hard, physical labor such as hunting, farming, chopping wood, smithing, tanning, or building. Interestingly enough, they didn't even cook. However, they did sew, weave, bake bread, milk cows, make cheese and butter, and brew beer and mead. Since these jobs were easier, they were also performed by children. In fact, children were considered adults when they turned ten, after which they began doing their fair share of work with the adults.

This division of labor stemmed from how Anglo-Saxons viewed men and women. It was a woman's duty to help the men after the battle and to keep them well fed and clothed. On the other hand, it was the man's duty to protect the women and their family in general as well as to provide for them with hard work.

In terms of marriage, women were allowed to leave as they pleased; however, the only recorded cases of marriage annulments were during adultery. Men would take control of a woman's property, but they were also obliged to give them something called the "morning gift," which was usually land and material goods. These would belong to her and her alone, and she was allowed to do whatever she wanted with it. In case of a divorce, a woman could leave a man, and she would usually get half of the property. A widow was not allowed to marry until a full year had passed. This might sound cruel, but it could also be seen as a way of letting the widow cope and, more importantly, make a later marriage decision with a clearer head. Once the twelve months were up, she could choose to marry (or not marry) whomever she wanted.

Sex work also existed during Anglo-Saxon England, and the prices for sex services varied based on who the client was (churls usually paid less than nobles). When it came to rape, women of all statuses were legally protected from it, and harsh punishments were exacted on the rapists themselves. However, there are written records of men advocating the beating of women, suggesting that there were either customs that damaged women in general or that this was an issue that needed to be resolved. Early Christianity strongly objected to beatings in general, so they couldn't have looked at this practice without condemnation.

Legally speaking, women had property rights and could stand witness to trials. They were also responsible for their own actions, and if slighted by the law, they were compensated personally. Most landowning women came from the upper classes, but even commoner women could inherit land, as written evidence within charters does not show that previous landowners preferred one gender over the other. When a woman inherited the land, she would get different items such as livestock, slaves, clothing, jewels, furnishings, and books along with it. They even got to keep tablecloths, wall hangings, and bed sheets since they were the ones to make them and were considered theirs.

Women would often be instrumental in certain political events in Anglo-Saxon England. It was Bertha, the wife of King Æthelberht, that was responsible for the king converting to Christianity and bringing it to England in the first place. She was a Merovingian princess, a daughter of Charibert I, and a devout Christian. Thanks to her, an old Roman church outside of Canterbury was restored and became her private chapel which she dedicated to St. Martin of Tours. This church would later become the Church of St. Martin, one of the oldest Anglo-Saxon churches in Canterbury and England as a whole. Bertha was venerated after her death, which happened sometime during the first decade of the 7th century. This makes her one of the first women canonized as saints in Britain.

Anglo-Saxon Art

People often get the impression that Anglo-Saxons were brutes who enjoyed war, killing, feasting, loud celebrations, and the occasional domestic violence. However, archeological evidence provides us with one more important aspect of Anglo-Saxon life. They were also very skilled artists with skills varying from metallurgy to manuscript illumination, from jewelry crafting to ivory carving, and from making elaborate tapestries to sculpting enormous monuments to their culture. A culture's art can give us a lot of insight into what they valued, how skilled they were with a particular craft, what materials and tools they used, and how their culture changed through the centuries.

Most of the artifacts found between sub-Roman Britain and Norman Britain show an affinity toward Christ and Christianity, which isn't all that strange considering that we now know how it developed throughout the centuries. Illuminated manuscripts are a perfect example of this. For the uninitiated reader, an illuminated manuscript is a religious document where the text has a lot of elaborate ornamentations, such as decorated initials, page borders, and even miniature illustrations. The materials used in such a practice were usually silver or gold; however, that's largely true for the Western Christian tradition of illumination.

The initial illuminated manuscripts combined a lot of different styles of this art, namely those of Germanic, Celtic, and Italian illumination. The Stockholm Codex Aureus is a perfect example of these mixtures of styles since its portrait is largely Italian (or rather tries to imitate the Italian style) while the letters themselves are insular in nature. Insular art, it should be noted, is an art style that developed in Britain and Ireland which is distinct from all other styles in mainland Europe. It's called insular because the term *insula* means "island."

There aren't a lot of manuscripts with elements of insular art in 9th-century Britain, but their elements can be seen in manuscripts from mainland Europe wherever the Anglo-Saxon missionaries did their work. For example, the Echternach Abbey in Luxembourg houses the famous Echternach Gospels, which were most likely illuminated in Northumbria. By the end of the 9th century, however, the so-called Winchester style of illumination was created and heavily used. Some distinctions of this style include agitated or wrinkled draperies, acanthus borders, and historiated initials. The best example of the late Winchester style illumination is the Benedictional of St. Æthelwold which actually drew from a few other styles, such as Byzantine and Carolingian illumination.

Producing goods from precious metals such as gold and silver, or even basic metals and alloys, was a practice the Anglo-Saxons actually did before Christianity. The most frequent examples of this practice are found before the 7th century, usually as round elaborate quoit brooches. Thanks to the discovery of the ship burial at Sutton Hoo, we know that these brooches, and indeed other metalwork, were highly developed at this time.

Brooches were far from the only items found and unearthed from the Anglo-Saxon period. Archeologists also found rings, coins, belt buckles, military fittings, and various other items. From written records, we also know that the metalworkers made statues, doors, shrines, and other large-scale metal pieces, but barely any of these survived to this day. The most likely reason for their disappearance is the constant Viking raids followed by the subsequent Norman invasion and other events. Unfortunately, looting was frequent during those raids, and the monasteries and churches, as the best-equipped places in England, had these items in abundance.

In terms of masters of metalwork, we have a few of the artists' names available to us from written accounts. One such artist was Spearhafoc, who would later become a Benedictine monk, an abbot, and Bishop-Elect of London. He was prominent in the mid-11th century and was renowned for his skills at goldsmithing, gold engraving, and painting. It's probably these skills that got him promoted so quickly to a high church position. Another artist of a similar status was Mannig of Evesham. Both artists have their lives documented and chronicled in their respective abbeys. Other artists are mentioned as well but mostly in passing.

A lot of these metalworks included scenes of animals in reeds or bushes carved onto the surface. But the Anglo-Saxons didn't just use metals to carve the scenes they wanted. More often than not, they would use ivory and other types of bone for equally elaborate efforts. For example, an entire casket, most likely carved in Northumbria in the 8th century, was made of whalebone, and it even has a riddle on it that hints as much. Artists actually imported a lot of these bones, especially the walrus bones, from the north. Other examples of ivory carvings include various scenes depicting Christ - either his birth, crucifixion, or different motifs from the Bible that included him.

But metal and ivory weren't enough. Anglo-Saxon stoneworkers even carved and shaped rocks, mostly to get massive outdoor crosses but sometimes to have an elaborate relief. These crosses would often combine both pagan and Christian elements, which is one of the reasons why they would be frequently destroyed or defaced during the Reformation. Many of these crosses actually survived in Ireland and can be seen today.

A cross would typically be very tall and slender, with some exceptions to this rule having been found in Mercia. Elements of Celtic paganism would often be there, such as vines and leaves. Moreover, there might be some hints that these crosses were originally painted, somewhat like Greek and Roman statues. The crosses themselves were popular at the time, especially when the Danish Vikings began to invade and when they finally took control in the late 10th and early 11th centuries. They began to "mass-produce" similar stone crosses, but they didn't have the same artistic quality of their Anglo-Saxon predecessors.

Textiles were equally popular "canvases" for contemporary Anglo-Saxon artists. They favored embroideries and tapestries, and many such works were made in early medieval England. Sadly, few survived, mainly because the material they were made from was reused in other works of art. Possibly the most famous example of Anglo-Saxon tapestries is the elaborate Bayeux Tapestry which depicts the Battle of Hastings. Of course, the tapestry itself was made within twenty years after the battle, but it is done in the style and manner of old Anglo-Saxon weavers. As we have established earlier, embroidery and other needlework were largely done by women. Therefore, we can safely assume that nuns and priestesses made the Bayeux Tapestry. Interestingly, some historians claim this work of art to be the first European version of a comic book because of its sequential storytelling nature.

Finer textile works incorporated silk and precious metal threads, namely gold and silver, as well as lots of precious gems, glass beads, and pearls. More often than not, these elaborate tapestries were owned by priests or royal families, and they were usually used in religious ceremonies.

The Anglo-Saxons also dabbled in other materials. For example, glass was very popular when it came to making luxury drinking glasses (like the claw beakers from the 6th and 7th centuries), glass beads, and church windows. Sometimes they would import glass workers from Francia, now known as France, but oftentimes, they would just rework old Roman glass items. Enamel was also often used instead of glass.

Then there's leather. Anglo-Saxon books would be bound in different types of covers. As we saw earlier, they could even be ornamented in ivory. Leather was one such material, and we have a famous example from the late 7th century to show us how skilled the craftsmen were at leather bookbinding. The stunning St Cuthbert Gospel is the oldest Western-bound book to remain unaltered to this very day. It has incised lines, elaborate relief decoration, and even some color. Naturally, the Anglo-Saxons didn't just use leather to bind books. Their leather artwork probably also covered belts, purses, and satchels, though we sadly don't have a lot of physical evidence of this, and the contemporary texts that talk about leather binding don't mention the more secular uses for leather ornamentation.

We can see that Anglo-Saxon artists had a wide range of skills and a wide range of materials. Of course, their missions to the continent also brought knowledge of illuminating manuscripts, carving figures, and working stones and fabrics. With that in mind, we can say that the insular art of Britain influenced a lot of early European Christian art styles. Even certain motifs became commonplace after the Anglo-Saxon missionaries began traveling Europe. For example, the elements of Christ's legs and feet alone being seen, the Hellmouth, St. John the Evangelist writing at the foot of a cross, Moses with horns, the depiction of the Last Judgment, and Mary Magdalene at the foot of the cross all originated in Anglo-Saxon Britain. These would become widely used in European art for the following centuries.

Winchester-style evangelist portrait, Grimbald Gospels, early 11th century[vii]

Written Works of the Anglo-Saxon Period

Pagan Anglo-Saxons didn't have an alphabet of their own that we know of. They were a pre-literate society, meaning they passed their knowledge onto their descendants by means of oral tradition. When Christianity came, literacy began to spread, but it was largely reserved for the higher classes. Though it wasn't impossible for a churl or a farmer to know how to read, it was almost exclusively the royal family and the priests that could afford to learn how to read and write. Churches were centers of the written word, though certain kings might have even hired private tutors for their children who also came from the clergy.

There is one major issue when it comes to Christianity and literacy in early medieval England. Namely, the priests who would preserve old Anglo-Saxon legends and myths would often dress them up in Christian undertones. That way, they could cloak the pagan elements and maintain a Christian narrative. Famous works such as *Beowulf* are a good example of this.

Anglo-Saxons enjoyed both poetry and prose. In terms of poetry, there were heroic poems and epics, elegies, adaptations of classical Latin poems, and riddles. The riddles, in particular, were exceptionally popular during this time, with 94 of them recorded in the Exeter Book, a lengthy compendium of Anglo-Saxon poetry. Christian poems became more and more popular with kingdoms slowly abandoning paganism, so biblical paraphrases, lives of saints, and even original poems appeared, with the most famous example being the *Dream of the Rood*.

In terms of epic poetry, Anglo-Saxon literature cannot be discussed without mentioning *Beowulf*. This epic, containing the exploits of the titular hero, was written down by an anonymous author sometime in the 10th century, though it was more than likely composed far earlier. Supernatural elements of Beowulf were explained away by adding Christian parallels, possibly by the very author who wrote it down since it was usually priests who dabbled in preserving poetry and prose. Numerous authors worked on translating it, including the famous fantasy author J. R. R. Tolkien who considered it a classic of English literature.

Most poems were written down anonymously. However, we do know the names of a few poets such as Cynewulf, Aldhelm, and Cædmon, the latter being known as the earliest English poet.

Prose was just as important during the development of Anglo-Saxon kingdoms. Both Christian and secular prose was prominent, with translations of Latin works being a notable practice at the time. Priests and monks would often write polemics, sermons, hagiographies, and other works that had powerful Christian themes, though they would often be written in Latin rather than Old English, at least in the early days of English Christianity. Two of the most famous prose writers of the Anglo-Saxon period in Britain were Gildas and the Venerable Bede. Gildas' polemic known as *De Excidio et Conquestu Britanniae* or *On the Ruin and Conquest of Britain* is the earliest source we have that gives us historical glimpses of Anglo-Saxon societies at the time. However, Gildas himself would often provide contradictory or outright incorrect information since his focus wasn't the historicity of events but rather the condemnation of the British in terms of Christian behavior. Bede, on the other hand, wrote his *Ecclesiastical History of the English People* with somewhat more historical accuracy. Born in Northumbria, he would, of course, have a bias toward that region. However, the events he describes, which largely focus on the history of Christian churches in England but also contains a lot of historical information on the early kingdoms and their political situations, can be retraced with a massive amount of accuracy. He is considered to be the first English historian despite his work not having that intention originally.

Of course, there are works that deal with history in a more secular way, such as the famed *Anglo-Saxon Chronicle*. Compiled by an unknown author, it contains information of about 300 years of English history. While this is an impressive feat, the *Chronicle* suffers from the same issues that other secular historical works do at the time. Namely, most of its sources are dubious or even outright taken from oral tradition, and some errors do occur in terms of dates and events. Some events were merely mentioned without any outcomes or listing the people involved. Battles would be described, but no place names given, kings listed, or victors and losers announced. Despite all of this, the *Anglo-Saxon Chronicle* remains an important part of Anglo-Saxon literary history.

Secular written works of Anglo-Saxons also dealt with mathematics, medicine, geography, language, and the law. Legal texts, in particular, would be bound in single volumes, detailing law codes of different kings and specific cases of legal disputes in various cities and towns. All in all, English prose, much like poetry, flourished during this time, despite the fact that it was limited to the upper classes.

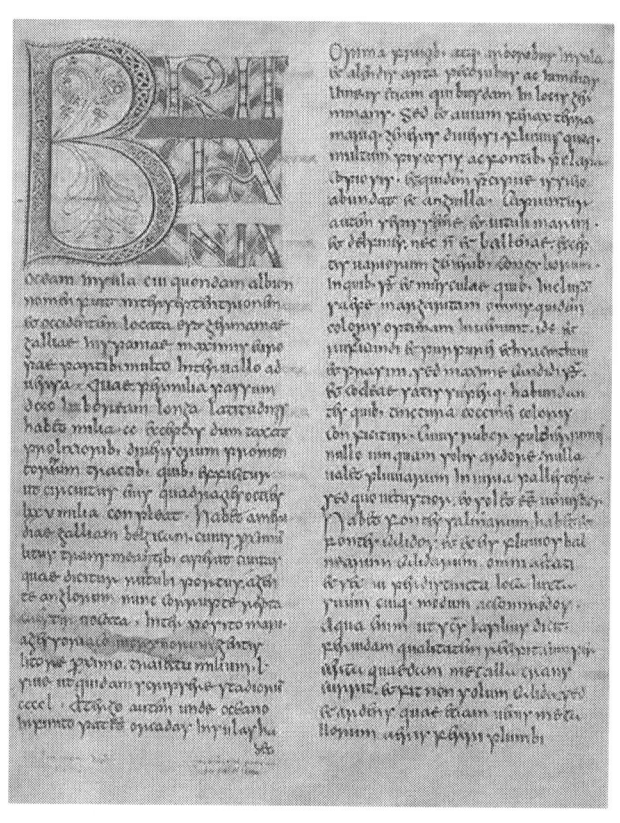

Folio 3v of St. Petersburg Bede[viii]

Chapter 5 – Anglo-Saxon Kingdoms

Before the Kings

Angles, Saxons, and Jutes were all tribal cultures. Their social hierarchy consisted of a ruler, a tribal council, priests, workers, and slaves, with more nuanced titles coming later. Once they began settling on British soil, they had two severe obstacles in their way. The first was the local Romans, whereas the second was the local Celtic people, the Britons. But even amongst themselves, these tribes didn't really work in unity. In fact, Bede, while addressing earlier accounts of these peoples by Gildas, openly states that the three groups are a "separate race." Jutes would inhabit Kent and the Isle of Wight. People that came from Saxony would be the ancestors of East Saxons, South Saxons, and West Saxons. And finally, Angles that moved to the island would be the forefathers of East and Middle Angles, Northumbrians, and Mercians.

Naturally, there were other Germanic tribes that raided the island and moved with the aforementioned three, but it's also important to note that Celtic tribes and entire Celtic kingdoms also held some local governance, if very minor. The North of Britain, roughly the area of today's Scotland, remained more or less isolated from any major Anglo-Saxon influence. In addition, as minor Celtic tribes got subjugated by the Anglo-Saxons, a few kingdoms held their own and moved west, eventually settling the territory of modern-day Wales. In terms of people groups, early medieval Britain was very diverse.

The Tribal Hidage

As stated in earlier chapters, a hide was an area of arable land that was enough to sustain a household. At some point in the early 7th century, a document was drawn up listing certain territories and how many hides they owned. The document doesn't have a contemporary title, but because of its contents, modern historians refer to it as the Tribal Hidage. As its name suggests, the Tribal Hidage lists over thirty tribes and how many hides of land they owned. Reading the document gives us a good glimpse of the ethnic and racial makeup of Britain at the time.

It should be noted, however, that the earliest examples of the Tribal Hidage we have come from the 11th century, at least four centuries after the original was written and lost to history. This is important because even with an earlier manuscript we can't be sure of how accurate it is. The more time there is between the original and the copy, which was made by hand and most certainly written by priests, the higher the chances are of it listing incorrect or incomplete, if not even biased, data.

Each tribe listed in the Tribal Hidage has a corresponding number of hides, which we will not reproduce here. We will, however, look at the tribal names and try to piece together who was who in early medieval Britain. The names are as follows:

1. Myrcna Landes
2. Wocensætna
3. Westerna
4. Pecsætna

5. Elmedsætna

6. Lindesfarona mid Hæthfeldlande (two territories counted as one)

7. Suth Gyrwa

8. North Gyrwa

9. East Wixna

10. West Wixna

11. Spalda

12. Wigesta

13. Herefinna

14. Sweordora

15. Gifla

16. Hicca

17. Withgara

18. Noxgaga

19. Ohtgaga

20. Hwinca

21. Cilternsætna

22. Hendrica

23. Unecung(a)ga

24. Arosaetna

25. Færpinga

26. Bilmiga

27. Widerigga

28. East Willa

29. West Willa

30. East Engle

31. East Sexena

32. Cantwarena

33. Suth Sexena

34. West Sexena

That is quite a few tribes, and among these are a few names we recognize. Immediately we can spot Mercia at the top, then East Angles, East and West Saxons, Kent (Cantwarena), and the Isle of Wight (Withgara). Other tribes are also recognizable to us from Bede's work, though we don't know much about them other than the fact that they had kings and some form of independence. Elmet, Hwicce, Lindsey, and Magonsaete (listed here under different names) all had royal houses that clashed with the other known Anglo-Saxons at the time, but some of these tribes like the Noxgaga and the Othgaga still elude historians. Even places like Suth Gyrwa only bring about speculation as we have no concrete evidence of similarly named Anglo-Saxon tribes in any other texts. Modern cartographers have compiled maps of probable locations of some of these tribes, and judging by them, we can safely say that the Anglo-Saxon tribes first occupied the eastern and southern areas of Britain.

Of course, this list is nowhere near extensive. There were more than likely other minor tribes settling close to these early Anglo-Saxon territories that are lost to time. More than likely they were either eradicated through war or simply assimilated with the dominant cultures of the emerging kingdoms. Some of these kingdoms might have been based on the old Roman units known as *civitates*, and kingdoms such as Kent, Lindsey, Deira, and Bernicia actually derive their names from the Latin terms for these territories.

The purpose of the Hidage itself isn't known to us. Considering the timing and the position of Mercia at the very beginning, it was likely issued by King Wulfhere of Mercia. At the time, he had control over several southern kingdoms, so a list like this would have been a handy tool to know how to tax them or have a good land overview in case of disputes. This text contains, bizarrely, a figure of 100,000 hides for Wessex. It is more than double the amount Mercia itself had, 30,000. This can indicate that later authors changed the numbers based on current states of the country. Namely, Wessex was expanding rapidly in the 11th century when our earliest copy of the Hidage was supposedly drafted. This huge number would go hand-in-hand with the kingdom's contemporary growth.

Bretwalda

Bretwalda is a term that usually translates to "ruler of Britain." It was used both by the Venerable Bede and the *Anglo-Saxon Chronicle* to distinguish rulers who held dominance over most of the island during the early days of Anglo-Saxon kings. This term might not have been used by contemporary Anglo-Saxon chroniclers, bishops, or members of the nobility, and it could have easily been a 9th-century name.

Bede lists seven kings that could be called a bretwalda of their time. Chronologically, they were Ælle of Sussex, Ceawlin of Wessex, Æthelberht of Kent, Rædwald of East Anglia, Edwin of Deira, Oswald of Northumbria, and Oswiu of Northumbria. The *Anglo-Saxon Chronicle* also adds one more ruler to the list, Egbert of Wessex, with Alfred of Wessex, also known as Alfred the Great, often being categorized with these rulers.

Neither Bede nor the *Chronicle* mention any Mercian rulers despite the fact that they held the same comparative level of power that the listed bretwalda did. Among these rulers are Penda, Wulfhere, Æthelred, Æthelbald, Offa, and Cœnwulf. The *Chronicle*'s anonymous author clearly had an anti-Mercian bias which would explain their exclusion from the list.

List of Kingdoms

Once again, we go back to George R. R. Martin. His own Aegon the Conqueror wanted a united Westeros, so he began conquering what was known as the Seven Kingdoms (of which he conquered six). Martin very clearly borrowed this number and this chain of events from early Anglo-Saxon history because, during the time of William the Conqueror, the island's politics were heavily reliant on the seven kingdoms that were active at the time. Collectively, their rule is called the Heptarchy, or the Rule of the Seven. There were, of course, minor kingdoms, and some of these minor kingdoms would even grow to create major ones, but we'll get to that shortly.

According to historians, the seven kingdoms of early medieval Britain, also known as petty kingdoms, were as follows: East Anglia, Northumbria, Mercia, Wessex, Sussex, Essex, and Kent. They would each come to dominate one another at certain points in history, but their unification was inevitable, even before William set foot in Britain.

East Anglia

As its name suggests, East Anglia was the kingdom primarily inhabited by the Angles. Its territory took up the modern-day counties of Suffolk and Norfolk, though historians suggest it stretched a bit farther than that.

In terms of the Tribal Hidage, East Anglia covered an area of 30,000 hides of land. They were ruled by the kings from the Wuffingas dynasty. In their early days, the Wuffingas were pagan, but with the coming of King Rædwald, they began the slow process of converting to Christianity.

Of course, East Anglia's history began much earlier than that. Somewhere around 450 CE, the Angles were already settling in the area, occupying the old Roman civitas of Venta Icenorum. As they slowly began to settle, their kings grew in power and slowly began to clash with other local rulers.

One interesting fact to note about East Anglia is that it was probably the first area in Britain where English was spoken, or rather Old English to be precise. This isn't a surprise considering that this area was one of the earliest Anglo-Saxon settlements in sub-Roman Britain. Linguists and scholars have studied place names, coin inscriptions, personal names, and old texts to uncover the linguistic background of the region. They discovered that East Anglian people had their own dialect just like the Mercian, the Kentish, the West Saxons, and the Northumbrians did. However, it's very hard to confirm this with any authority considering that we literally have no written sources from that era that directly come from East Anglia.

We can't emphasize enough how sad it is that no documents, such as wills or charters, survived that were written by the East Angles. Even their direct history, such as the list of kings and battles, come to us from outside sources such as the Venerable Bede and the *Anglo-Saxon Chronicle*. Based on the limited information that we have, we can confirm a few basic facts. The Wuffingas ruled over East Anglia until 749 when their last king died. After that, they either fell to Mercian rule or to the rule of kings whose lineage our history doesn't recognize. By the early 9th century, East Anglia had regained its independence, and not long after they did, the Vikings began their raids. Like a lot of eastern kingdoms, East Anglia was incorporated into the Danelaw, a common name for the parts of England that were under direct Danish or Viking rule, only to be reclaimed by Edward the Elder several decades later. The final decades of East Anglia were filled with political turmoil as ownership of it shifted from Anglo-Saxons to Danes. The last known Danish ruler over the region was Cnut the Great, who appointed Thorkell the Tall to rule as earl of East Anglia in 1017.

Notable East Anglian Kings

The only East Anglian dynasty we have data on were the Wuffingas. They claimed to be the descendants of Wuffa, a semi-mythological king, and their name in Old English means "the children of the wolf." Wuffa might have ruled in the late 6th century if he was a historical king. Most sources mention him as the father of Tytila, the grandfather of Rædwald, and the founder of the dynasty; however, some sources claim that another ruler preceded him, namely his supposed father, Wehha.

Rædwald of East Anglia

Rædwald was, without a doubt, the most famed of all East Anglian kings. He ruled the kingdom from c. 599 to c. 624. He was by no means the only powerful ruler of this time period. Æthelberht of Kent was already in power when Rædwald ascended the throne and had, in fact, married Bertha at least a decade and a half prior. Other kings that were in power at the time were Ceolwulf of Wessex, Æthelfrith of Bernicia, and possibly Pybba, who supposedly founded Mercia in 585.

Rædwald reigned for 25 years. During that time, according to Bede, he was an overlord of several southern kingdoms and the fourth bretwalda. His early years marked him as a pagan king, but when Augustine landed in Kent, he traveled south to the court of King Æthelberht. Once there, Rædwald and another king, Saeberht of Essex, were baptized, and each of their kingdoms received bishoprics. This would make Rædwald the first Anglian king to convert to Christianity. His son, Eorpwald, had also converted, though he did this much later in life. However, once he ascended the throne after Rædwald's death in c. 624, he was usurped and killed by a pagan noble called Ricberht. This same noble might have even ruled over East Anglia for a few years before the Wuffingas reclaimed the throne, with the region falling back to paganism as Kent did after the death of King Æthelberht a decade earlier.

Rædwald effectively became an overlord of the nearby kingdoms after the death of King Æthelberht. We don't know a lot about the details of the early years of his reign. However, possibly the greatest historical event that involved the East Anglian king and that we know of was the deposition of Edwin of Northumbria and the Battle of the River Idle.

Edwin was not really the king of Northumbria. He was actually born in Deira, one of the two kingdoms that would make up the new land called Northumbria. The second kingdom, Bernicia, was ruled by Æthelfrith who wanted to depose and ultimately kill Edwin. He took control of both kingdoms in c. 604. Edwin was exiled and sought refuge in several different kingdoms such as the Celtic Gwynedd, Mercia, and, finally, East Anglia.

Initially, Rædwald received the exiled Edwin and refused to sell him out to Æthelfrith. However, after multiple attempts by the Bernician and Deiran king, Rædwald caved, which, according to written sources, his pagan wife shamed him for. It was supposedly because of this shaming that Rædwald, alongside Rægenhere, his son, and Edwin of Deira, faced Æthelfrith in the Battle of the River Idle in either 616 or 617. The resulting clash was so bloody that it became ingrained in the English collective memory, with the phrase "the river Idle was foul with the blood of Englishmen" still looming today. Rædwald lost his son that day, but he managed to kill the Bernician king and destroy his troops. Edwin was then crowned the king of the new kingdom, Northumbria, while Rædwald became the first king to have significant influence in politics of a separate independent kingdom. The king himself ruled uncontested until 624 when he died, and his son Eorpwald took the throne. Historians argue that the princely burial at Sutton Hoo, with its massive boat and elaborate gifts, was that of Rædwald himself. Some speculate that his son was either buried next to it in a smaller mound, or that he was the one buried in the boat and not his father. However, we don't have any written or archeological evidence to corroborate either option.

Anna of East Anglia

Don't let the name fool you; Anna was very much a man. Sometimes recorded as Onna, this king was the nephew of Rædwald and the son of Eni, making him one of the Wuffingas. He succeeded Ecgric, his relative from the same family, though we don't know exactly what their relationship was; they could have been brothers, cousins, or something else entirely.

Anna was famously praised by Bede for being a good Christian. All of his children, one son and either three or four daughters, were canonized as saints. Thanks to his influence, Cenwalh of Wessex converted as well during his exile in East Anglia.

Anna was also famous for securing political marriages of his daughters. Seaxburh, his oldest daughter, was married to Eorcenberht of Kent, allying the two kingdoms. In 652, he married his second daughter Æthelthryth to Tondberct of South Gyrwe. Anna himself was married to a noblewoman called Sæwara.

During Anna's reign, Penda of Mercia became a powerful monarch. In 651, the Mercian king attacked the monastery of Cnobheresburg, forcing Anna into exile. Two years later, he returned to East Anglia, but soon after, East Anglian and Mercian forces would clash at Bulcamp. Both Anna and his only son Jurmin were killed in the battle, leaving his brother, Æthelhere, as the successor to the throne.

Other Notable Kings of East Anglia

Among the Wuffingas, other notable kings include Sigeberht, Ealdwulf, and Ælfwald. Sigeberht was the first English king to be educated and baptized before he ascended the throne. In addition, he probably didn't rule alone but shared the kingly duties with his cousin Ecgric. After his abdication, Ecgric would continue to rule alone. Ealdwulf was the son of Æthelric and a grandson of Eni, and his reign is known for being uncharacteristically peaceful and prosperous, mainly because Gipeswic (today's Ipswich) was expanding at the time. His death in 713 brought Ælfwald to the throne, and he would rule for 36 years, with his reign being equally peaceful and prosperous. During his time, coin minting expanded and trade with continental Europe bloomed. Since there are no records of a direct heir, and because of conflicting information over who ruled East Anglia after his death, we can safely say that Ælfwald was the last of the Wuffingas to sit on the East Anglian throne.

Kent

Aside from the Isle of Wight, Kent is the only Anglo-Saxon kingdom that we know of which was populated largely by Jutes. It was also the first territory on British soil where Anglo-Saxons converted to Christianity. It's also interesting to note that Kent claimed direct descendancy from the legendary Hengist and Horsa.

Late 6th century Kent had a lot going for it. They were already having marital connections with the Merovingians from Francia. In fact, the Frankish kings probably held dominion over the region as early influences of the kingdom can be seen in Kentish artifacts. Kent even established regular trade, and in the following century, Kentish influence was also present in other European kingdoms and territories, such as Rhineland, Thuringia, Frisia, and Western Normandy.

However, marital relations were key here. They weren't just done out of a sense of love or duty; they were very much a powerful political tool in securing allies and growing one's influence. Æthelberht of Kent, though a pagan, married a Christian woman from the Merovingian dynasty and daughter to Charibert I named Bertha. It was thanks to this couple that Christianity began to spread in England, and it would be the bishops of Æthelberht that gave the Angles their first Christian king in Rædwald of East Anglia.

Sadly, Kent would not retain its glory for long. In the later years of the 7th century, both Northumbria and Mercia grew in power. It would ultimately be Mercian kings that would dominate Kent by the end of the century, though this wouldn't last long. There is evidence that Canterbury, at least, was still a powerful urban center, as both it and Rochester still had mints, producing the silver currency known as *sceattas* (singular: sceat).

As the 9th century rolled by, Wessex held supremacy over the other kingdoms, and Kent was in disarray. The Viking attacks of the next few centuries didn't really help as the raids left the kingdom in ruins. Thorkell the Tall himself led the raid of Canterbury in 1011, decimating the city. By the time William of Normandy came to conquer England, Kent had nowhere near as much power as it did in its early days.

Notable Kings of Kent

Æthelberht of Kent

Possibly the best-known ruler of this kingdom, Æthelberht ascended the throne in c. 589 and ended his reign when he died on February 24th, 616. He was regarded as the third bretwalda according to the *Anglo-Saxon Chronicle* and Bede. During his reign, he was the first pagan Anglo-Saxon king to allow Christianity to be openly practiced within his realm, personally inviting a mission from Rome in 597.

During his early reign, he held overlordship over the East Saxons and successfully converted his nephew, Sæberht of Essex, to Christianity. Similar to Rædwald, who had become the first Anglian Christian king, Sæberht would become the first Saxon Christian king. From his relationship with these two kings, we can ascertain that Kent held at least nominal dominion over Essex and East Anglia. Mercia was probably also under Æthelberht's domain, though this isn't backed by enough archeological or historical evidence.

Æthelberht was known for his efforts to Christianize his people. However, he was also known for his code of law, the oldest such document in any Germanic society of the Middle Ages. These laws covered punishments and compensations for personal slights and were divided by social classes. British historian Patrick Wormald had divided the laws into nine sections. The first section dealt with compensation for the clergy, the second for the king and his direct dependents, the third for earls (ealdormen), the fourth for churls, the fifth for the semi-free men, the sixth for personal injuries, the seventh for women, the eighth for servants, and the ninth for slaves. Usually, they would be compensated with money, such as shillings or the sceattas. One thing we do not know is why this code was written in the first place. One possible reason might be that Æthelberht wanted to "civilize" his people after they had accepted Christianity, the religion of both the Roman Church and their superior Merovingian rulers and next of kin. Issuing this code of law would not only make Æthelberht the first king to "import" Christianity in Britain but also one of its first, if not the first, lawmakers.

It is also speculated by historians that Æthelberht's reign saw the first coins minted in Britain, or rather the first coins that weren't Roman. There is no hard, physical evidence of this, though coins were already in use during the reign of his son and heir Eadbald, and Æthelberht himself does mention shillings in his code of law.

Æthelberht's death in 616 showed just how influential of a monarch he was. His son is said to have refused baptism and, to the Church's shock and condemnation, married his stepmother. Roughly at the same time, the East Saxon king Sæberht, the first Saxon king to receive baptism and next of kin to Eadbald, also died, and his three pagan sons took the throne. Kentish Christian missionaries were expelled from both kingdoms, signifying both a revolt against Christianity and the overlordship of Kent. Æthelberht's hard work seems to have been for nothing, at least at the time.

Wihtred of Kent

Wihtred ascended the throne around 690 CE after a period full of instability and no clear rulers in Kent. Most of the kingdoms were effectively under Mercian overlordship at this time, and Wihtred's predecessor, his father Ecgberht, died back in 673 when both of his sons were barely toddlers.

Until 692, Wihtred ruled jointly with another Kentish co-ruler called Swæfheard, after which he might have ruled alongside his son, Æthelberht II. During his early years as a king, Wihtred made peace with Ine of Wessex. Ine's predecessor, King Cædwalla, had previously conquered Kent and installed a puppet king named Mul who was burned to death by the Kentish common folk. Ine paid compensation for the deed, while Wihtred probably gave him some land in return.

Wihtred was also a known lawmaker. While the date isn't known for certain, historians suggest that late 695 was the year when Wihtred finalized his code, with Ine of Wessex doing the same a year earlier, suggesting that the two monarchs worked together in their years of peace. The laws themselves deal mostly in ecclesiastical affairs. Of its 28 chapters, only the final four have nothing to do with the Church. Reading through the laws, we can assume that the Church was given a lot of privileges and enjoyed a high position in society. Pagan beliefs were still around, though practicing them resulted in severe penalties, according to Wihtred's laws.

Statue of Æthelberht of Kent, interior of Rochester Cathedral[ix]

Eadberht III Præn

Not a whole lot is known of this king, but what we do know is that he ruled from 796 to 798 and was the last king of an independent Kent. He came into power directly after the death of Offa of Mercia, who had controlled Kent directly before he died. Before that, Eadberht was in exile enjoying Charlemagne's protection. His reign wasn't long, as merely two years after his ascension, the Mercian king Cœnwulf sacked Kent and captured him. Depending on the sources, Eadberht was either blinded and had his hands cut off or was released by Cœnwulf as a token of goodwill. Whatever the case might be, Eadberht was the last ruler of Kent that wasn't a puppet king.

Other Notable Kings of Kent

Much of Kent's history after Æthelberht includes kings from other houses, such as Mul. Mul was installed as king by his brother, Cædwalla of Wessex, in 686 after their joint conquest of Kent and the Isle of Wight. But reports state that the very next year, the Kentish rebelled against Mul and burned him as a result. Following Mul, there were several "joint reigns" that included Kings Swæfheard, Oswine, Swæfberht, and Wihtred. Not all of these rulers were from Kent as some had family ties with Wessex and Essex. Finally, we should mention Baldred of Kent. He ruled over the kingdom from 823 to possibly 827, and he's interesting to historians because it's not clear whether he was a puppet king of Mercia or the actual last Kentish-born king to be on the throne.

Essex

Essex is the modern name of the kingdom of the East Saxons. The territory of this small kingdom spanned from East Anglia to Kent and from Mercia to the North Sea. From what we can gather, several tribes existed in this area before they merged into one large kingdom. Those people included the Rodings, the Uppingas, the Haeferingas, the Haemele, the Berecingas, the Ginges, the Denge, and the Vange. Their kingdom came to be in the early 6th century, and like several other pagan Saxon tribes, the kings of future Essex claimed that Woden was their direct ancestor.

Sadly, there aren't a lot of written records or archeological evidence for us to piece together what Essex was like during the time of other Anglo-Saxon kingdoms. We only know that they had been subjugated at multiple points by bigger, more powerful regional kingdoms such as Mercia, East Anglia, or Kent.

Throughout their existence, the East Saxons had strong ties to the kings of Kent. Æthelberht's insistence on converting his nephew Sæberht to Christianity had an instrumental role in this, as the royal families continued supporting each other and intermarrying even during Mercian dominance. At one point in the 8th century, Essex began minting coins, possibly as a way of asserting their independence from other kingdoms. Mercia would eventually take control of Essex, but in the late 9th century, it would become incorporated into the Danelaw. Once Edward the Elder retook the territory from the Danes, the ruler of Essex was styled as an ealdorman rather than a king. From that point until William's conquest, Essex was little more than a shire.

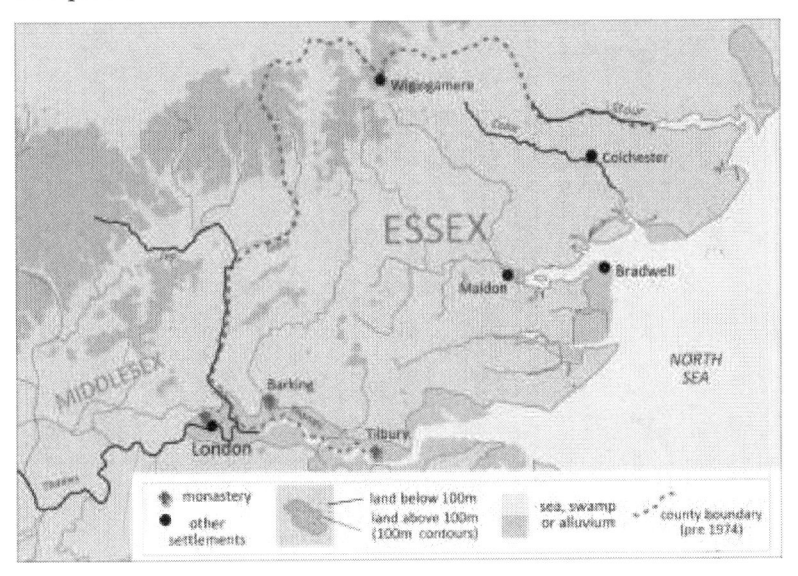

Map of Anglo-Saxon Essex[x]

Notable Kings of Essex

Sæberht of Essex

Sæberht ascended to the throne in c. 604, following his father, Sledd. Within the year, he converted to Christianity at Kent. However, all of his sons remained pagan, which led to problems after his death in c. 616. During the same time, Mellitus, a member of the Gregorian mission to Canterbury, was made the first Bishop of London.

Not much is known about Sæberht's life. He had family ties in Kent, and the two kingdoms remained close even after his passing. Sæberht himself was the son of Sledd, who might have been the founder of the first dynasty of Essex, though we can't know this with certainty. During his time, London and Colchester were part of Essex, and London, in particular, was still a key city within the kingdom, retaining this position from Roman times. Within London, King Æthelberht built the old St Paul's church, possibly on the same spot where the current St Paul's Cathedral is located. This shows that while Sæberht ruled Essex in his own right, his uncle still held dominion over him. After all, London was not in Kent, nor a direct part of it, during Sæberht's reign.

Sæberht's death resulted in events similar to those of his uncle's death in Kent. Mellitus, still the Bishop of London, was exiled from the city by Sæberht's sons. All three sons were pagan, and according to legend, they exiled Mellitus because he refused to allow them to taste sacramental bread. Whatever the case may be, Essex was no longer a safe haven for Christians, at least in the early 7th century.

The Prittlewell site in the county of Essex contains an elaborate and possibly royal Anglo-Saxon tomb. Some archeologists speculate that Sæberht might have been buried here. Others claim that it is actually the resting place of his grandson, Sigeberht the Good, who was also a Christian king.

Sigeberht the Good

Ascending the throne around 653, Sigeberht ruled Essex for seven years until he was murdered by his kinsmen. Unlike his grandfather, the first Christian king of the East Saxons, we know quite a few details of Sigeberht's life.

Unlike his father and his kinsmen before him, Sigeberht converted to Christianity, though he did this at the urging of his friend, King Oswiu of Bernicia. He was baptized at one of Oswiu's estates by Bishop Finan. In his later years, Sigeberht would ask for Oswiu's help in reconverting the East Saxons into Christians. A monk called Cedd led the mission with a few other monks and went to Essex, having previously finished missionary work with the Middle Angles. Later in life, Cedd would become Bishop of Essex. Churches and

Christian communities were slowly emerging in Essex again, and the kingdom looked like it was going back to Christianity.

Sadly, Sigeberht's brothers (whom Bede doesn't mention by name when retelling this event) did not agree with his new religion. The king's murder might have had two well-known culprits, however. One would be his cousin Swithhelm, son of Seaxbald, while the other was Swithhelm's brother Swithfrith. Bede portrays this murder as if the kinsmen killed Sigeberht for his beliefs, but there's reason to believe that more complex politics of succession were involved. After the king's death, Swithhelm took the throne and ruled for the next four years.

Other Notable Kings of Essex

Considering how little we know about the kings of Essex, it's interesting to see that two separate rulers are noted as the progenitors of their royal dynasty. The first of these is Æscwine. We know next to nothing of this king other than a few name variants, though his name would suggest some Jutish, probably Kentish influence. His supposed son, Sledd, the father of Sæberht, is also considered by a few scholars to be the rightful founder of the house of Essex. Much like his brother, we know very little about Sledd. He might have married Ricula, the sister of Æthelberht, the king of Kent, and their son would have become the first East Saxon Christian king. However, Sledd also had another son, Seaxa, of whom we only know the name of.

Another king of note is Sigered of Essex. He ascended the throne in 798 and ruled until 825. However, he was both the last king and the last native ruler of Essex. This is explained by the fact that he had only been king until 812. Pressured by his Mercian overlords, he was no longer king but merely a duke. As a duke, he ruled over Essex until 825 when he ceded his kingdom. Essex then went to a different ruler, Ecgberht of Wessex.

Sussex

The South Downs are a range of chalk hills that contain a particularly large, prominent feature, that of Highdown Hill. As a settlement, it was inhabited well before Romans ever set foot there, but it's also an important site to research Anglo-Saxon history. Namely, around 450 CE, it housed a noticeable Anglo-Saxon cemetery which yielded a lot of interesting glass artifacts. This region would become home to the South Saxons, the tribe and later kingdom which we probably know the least about in terms of actual history.

The date brought up here is important because the South Saxons at the time traced their lineage to the landing of their earliest ancestor which, if they were to be believed, occurred more than two decades after the cemetery was in use. Chronologically speaking, that makes no sense, though the story they tell, one of battles and conquest, might have happened in those days, but since it was the time before Anglo-Saxons could read or write, we have nothing to corroborate it.

Sussex is the southernmost kingdom of the Anglo-Saxon Heptarchy. It used to lay well below Kent and had more than likely been a pagan kingdom well into the 7th century. Allied with Mercians against Wessex, the South Saxon kings would maintain their independence, and their king, Æthelwealh, converted to Christianity in 661 CE. He even invited a missionary, Wilfrid of Northumbria, to convert and preach to his subjects from 681 to 686 CE. Despite this alliance, the South Saxons would continue to be harassed by the West Saxons well into the 8th century. Sussex lost its independence to Offa of Mercia, however, around 770, though it seems to have made a bit of a comeback by the end of the century. At long last, at around 825 after the Battle of Ellendun, Wessex claimed Sussex for themselves, and from then onwards, the kingdom was no longer a kingdom but land ruled by dukes and ealdormen. Some of these would play prominent roles in the following centuries, especially during the wars against the Danelaw and the political scene before the Norman conquest.

Sussex was, from archeological evidence, a thriving community both during its heyday and while under foreign rule. Like other kingdoms that surrounded it, Sussex minted its own coins, with variations of these coins found dating back to the 8th century. In addition to minting, Sussex also flourished in trade and agriculture, as well as herding. The town of Lewes, in particular, had a rich history in trading, farming, and herding.

In terms of law, several place names such as Tinhale, Madehurst, and Ditchling suggest that the early South Saxons took part in folkmoots, where groups of free men presided over by the nobles would discuss the items of the day or settle disputes. There was no real governing body, and proper practice of law didn't happen until the Christianization of Sussex in the 7th century. In the 10th century when they were under Wessex rule, several witena gemōts took place in Sussex, most notably the one in 930 and the one during the reign of King Æthelstan, probably held at Hamsey.

Notable Kings of Sussex

Æthelwealh of Sussex

Æthelwealh lived during the time of Wulfhere of Mercia and is the first Sussex king whose existence history can confirm. We don't know when he was born, but we know he probably took the throne c. 660 CE. Before he did that, however, he traveled to Mercia to meet Wulfhere since the earlier years of this century saw the two kingdoms join a political union of sorts. While in Mercia, Æthelwealh was baptized with Wulfhere presiding as a sponsor. This act made Æthelwealh the first Christian South Saxon king. However, the rest of Sussex wouldn't be baptized until roughly two decades later. One more detail regarding Wulfhere and Æthelwealh that we know of is the Mercian king's gift of the Isle of Wight to the South Saxon king in 661, which had previously been either independent or under Kentish control.

In 681, stricken by famine, the Saxon people were visited by St. Wilfrid of Northumbria. He was there on a mission to convert them, and evidently, he did a good job of it, teaching the hungry Saxons how to fish so they wouldn't go hungry. While this story is apocryphal at best, we do know that Æthelwealh gave Wilfrid 87 hides as a gift for his efforts, and Wilfrid, with the royal vill, comparable to a manor or parish, Æthelwealh also gave him, founded the Selsey Abbey which would remain the center of the Sussex bishopric until William the Conqueror came and claimed Sussex.

Wilfrid, however, wasn't too loyal to the South Saxon king. When he met with Cædwalla of Wessex sometime after the baptism of the South Saxons, the two reached an agreement to further their own interests by working together against Æthelwealh. Both the priest and the prince were exiles from their kingdoms, though Cædwalla would later become the king of Wessex for three years. During Æthelwealh's reign, Cædwalla was in charge of a tribe called Gewisse. In 685, he killed Æthelwealh and took the throne of Sussex by force. Unfortunately for him, he didn't keep it long, as two of Æthelwealh's ealdormen named Berhthun and Andhun chased him out. During that same year, Cædwalla would come to rule Wessex.

Æthelwealh wasn't nearly as well documented as other contemporary kings. He was nevertheless an instrumental ruler in bringing Christianity to the South Saxons of Britain. He was also one of the earliest rulers to recognize how powerful of an ally Mercia could be, as his alliance with Wulfhere proved to be a fruitful one. We also know that he had at least some form of an alliance with a minor kingdom called Hwicce, considering he took Eafe, the daughter of King Eanfrith, as his queen. We don't know if the marriage produced any heirs though.

Other Notable Kings of Sussex

No list of Sussex kings would be complete without mentioning the supposed progenitor of their noble line. According to legend, Ælle of

Sussex first landed on the shores of Britain in 477. After he and his three sons—Cymen, Wlencing, and Cissa—came to the island, they began slaughtering some of the local Britons. The year 485 would also supposedly see Ælle's victory over the local Celtic people at a place called Mearcred's Burn. Then, in 491, he besieged a place called Andredes cester with his son Cissa and, yet again, committed genocide of the Celts. Though a pagan, Ælle was celebrated as one of the greatest South Saxon kings to have lived.

Of course, Ælle's timeline of events doesn't match up with the archeological findings at Highdown Hill. In fact, it's even difficult to trace whether he actually existed at all. Nevertheless, Bede and the *Anglo-Saxon Chronicle* both mention him as the first bretwalda to rule over the Anglo-Saxon tribes of his area.

Northumbria

Its name is a dead giveaway when it comes to its geographical position. Northumbria was the northernmost kingdom of the Anglo-Saxons, though it didn't initially start out as a single kingdom. During the Christianization of the Anglo-Saxons, its territory was home to two smaller but equally influential kingdoms, those of Deira and Bernicia. Their common name after unification, Northumbria, comes from them being north of the Humber estuary on the east coast of Britain. It's possible that Bede was the first to actually coin the term and that the kings of united Northumbria merely styled themselves "king of Bernicia and Deira."

Of the two, Deira was closer to the Humber, bordering Bernicia at the river Tees. To the west, Deira bordered the edge of the Vale of York, and of course, York itself was the capital. Bernicia extended from Tees to the river Forth. Its own capital was the city of Bamburgh, which would become the only remaining independent earldom of the region in the 9th century before it was ultimately absorbed by England and Scotland years later.

It's difficult to keep track of all the kings that ruled Northumbria mainly because the dynasties of the two kingdoms constantly shifted. A member of Bernicia's royal line would take the throne of Deira only to be replaced a generation later by a ruler from Deira, who in turn would take Bernicia's throne as well. Nevertheless, the kingdom gave Britain no less than three kings that would be named bretwalda by Bede and the *Anglo-Saxon Chronicle*.

It's important to note that we have more information about Northumbria than on all the other kingdoms. Bede himself was Northumbrian, so it's safe to say that he had a clear bias in choosing which kingdoms he wanted to discuss in more detail. For example, he talks very little about Mercians and West Saxons because those two held the same level of power that Northumbria once had. It would also explain why he didn't include any Mercians and only one West Saxon king when he talked about the bretwalda of the island. Nevertheless, his insight gives us plenty of information on how this northernmost kingdom grew, expanded, and interacted with others.

Notable Northumbrian Kings

Before we move on with this section, it's important to note that not all of these kings styled themselves as unified rulers. Sometimes a ruler would only reign over Deira or Bernicia, then get deposed by a different ruler, and later become reinstated to the throne with a different title. For the sake of simplicity, we will treat these rulers as kings of Northumbria rather than rulers of either Bernicia, Deira, or both kingdoms with both names intact within the titles.

Æthelfrith of Bernicia

Æthelfrith was in power during the early 7th century. Before he became the ruler of Bernicia, he was already known for his military successes against the Celtic Britons. The Bernician king kept pushing the Britons farther west, securing more and more land for himself. In circa 604, he exiled Edwin and took the throne of Deira. While not officially uniting the two kingdoms, he was their ruler until the day he died, a little over a decade later.

Other notable events of Æthelfrith's life include the famous Battle of Chester against the Kingdom of Powys and his slaughtering of monks at Bangor-Is-Coed. Both events happened somewhere between 613 and 616 CE. During the Battle of Chester, Æthelfrith's forces crushed several Celtic kings, as well as kings of other Anglo-Saxon countries such as Mercians. The king of Powys was killed in battle, as was another king whose name we know but cannot recognize historically.

It was the slaughter of monks that left a particular impression on Bede when he wrote about Æthelfrith of Bernicia. According to him, the monks of Bangor-Is-Coed did nothing but pray when Æthelfrith's forces arrived. He saw this as impudence, so he had over a thousand monks killed. Some fifty or so managed to escape. Whatever his reasoning behind this act was, both the slaughter of monks and the Battle of Chester managed to separate the Celtic people from the north from those in the southwest.

Æthelfrith's reign wouldn't last long after these events. Edwin, with the help of Rædwald, hid in East Anglia after moving from one kingdom to the next during his exile. Apparently, Rædwald was offered compensation several times by Æthelfrith to give up Edwin, and though the king of East Anglia eventually agreed, his queen shamed him into taking up arms instead. Æthelfrith died at the Battle of the River Idle, leaving the throne of Deira and Bernicia vacant for Edwin to claim.

Edwin

Edwin was the son of Ælle, the first historically known king of Deira. Shortly after his father's death, however, a different ruler, Æthelfrith, took the throne. While in exile, Edwin married for the first time to a woman called Cwenburg, the daughter of the Mercian king Ceorl. With the help of the East Anglian king Rædwald, Edwin deposed Æthelfrith and took control of both his native Deira and Bernicia. This was irregular because most of the kings that ruled over both kingdoms were from the Bernician ruling house.

Edwin slowly expanded his territory and made important changes. His second marriage was to Æthelburg, the sister of the ruler of Kent, Eadbald, a dear friend of Edwin's. Since Kent had been undergoing massive conversions to Christianity, it was only a matter of time before the new religion began sprouting roots in Northumbria. Edwin himself was baptized in 627 CE.

In terms of expansion, Edwin took hold of eastern Mercia, the Isle of Man, and Anglesey. While he wasn't a particularly decisive king during the life of Rædwald, he more than earned the title of bretwalda in his later years. In 629, he supposedly defeated Cadwallon ap Cadfan, the king of Gwynedd and his possible foster brother. For nearly half a decade, nobody would challenge Edwin until the Battle of Hatfield Chase in 633. Cadwallon and Penda of Mercia defeated and killed the Northumbrian king. According to some written accounts, his body was first hidden in Edwinstowe, an event the place got its name from. His head was later taken to York and buried, while the rest of his body was buried at Whitby. Edwin was venerated as a saint, with his cult slowly but firmly developing in Northumbria at the time.

After Edwin's death, his successors reverted to paganism, and there was massive infighting. Cadwallon was still a threat, but a different Northumbrian ruler was going to put an end to him very soon.

Portrait of St. Edwin of Northumbria, St. Mary, Siedmere, Yorkshire[xi]

Oswald

Oswald was a Bernician prince and the son of Æthelfrith. When his father was killed and Edwin came to power, Oswald was in exile, traveling different kingdoms and learning Irish in the meantime. Once he came back to Bernicia, he battled King Cadwallon at Heavenfield and destroyed his army, despite having fewer soldiers on his side. Cadwallon had previously also killed Oswald's brother, Eanfrith, who ruled Bernicia for a very short period of time. Oswald's victory brought him honor and recognition, so his next step was very clear.

Shortly after his victory over the combined forces of Gwynedd and Mercia, Oswald was crowned king of Bernicia and Deira, the first king after Edwin to do so and the second Bernician king to hold the throne. He was later known as a bretwalda himself, possibly taking control of the kingdom of Lindsey and the people of Goddodin.

Christianity also played a big part during Oswald's reign. After his kingdom had relapsed into paganism, he decisively began to take active steps to reinstall the faith in Christ. With the assistance of an Irish priest named Aidan, the conversion took place sometime before 635 when Aidan became a bishop. Oswald himself would be venerated as a priest after his death, with his cult growing so strong that it overshadowed that of Edwin, his Deiran predecessor.

Oswald would ultimately die during the Battle of Maserfield. His army lost to Penda of Mercia, and Oswald was killed and cut up into pieces with his limbs mounted on spikes. This happened in 641 or 642, and the consequences of this battle were the fortification of Penda's power in the south and political turmoil in Northumbria.

Oswiu

Oswiu was Oswald's brother who took the Bernician throne because the rightful heir, Oswald's son Œthelwald, was underage. During his early years, he married the Deiran princess Eanflæd, though she would be merely his first wife. Sadly, this marital union did not help him maintain any control over Deira, which at the time was ruled by a different king, Oswine.

Around 651, Oswiu and Oswine were set to engage in battle, but according to Bede, Oswine sent his troops home and was later betrayed and murdered by one of his own in Oswiu's name. As compensation for his death, Oswiu went to Gilling and established an abbey there where people could say prayers for both kings. Œthelwald, the son of Oswald and potential rightful heir of the Bernician throne, was given the rule of Deira instead.

Another ruler that Oswiu managed to dispose of was Penda of Mercia. Penda's influence grew stronger during this period, and he was effectively the bretwalda, even though the written sources omit all Mercians who fit the title. The rivalry between Oswiu and Penda escalated at the Battle of the Winwaed in 655. Penda lost the battle and was killed. Considering he was a pagan king, Oswiu's victory effectively ended paganism in Anglo-Saxon England.

Oswiu would become a powerful bretwalda in his own right. His influence was felt in Mercia, Kent, and possibly even parts of Wales.

Mercian King Wulfhere eventually rose up against Oswiu, but Oswiu must have been too powerful to beat through sheer force, so they settled their grievances with diplomacy. This event occurred sometime between 657 and 659.

The Northumbrian king remained a powerful figure until his death in 670. His son Ecgfrith was his successor in Bernicia, while Deira was ruled by his other son Ælfwine.

Other Notable Kings of Northumbria

Ælla and Ida were the first known rulers of Deira and Bernicia, respectively. The descendants of Ælla even claimed that he traced his ancestry all the way back to Woden. Two more notable kings that would come to rule Deira were Osric and his son, Oswine. Osric and another ruler, Eanfrith of Bernicia, were deemed to be the worst rulers of that time in Northumbria, as they reverted back to paganism and barely kept their two kingdoms together. Osric was killed by Cadwallon at some point, after which his son Oswine became king. He ruled until 651 when his friend Earl Humwald betrayed him by delivering him to Oswiu's soldiers who executed him, helping Oswiu take a firmer hold of Deira.

Mercia

Perhaps unfairly treated by writers of contemporary sources, Mercia was one of the greatest powers in Anglo-Saxon Britain, producing several monarchs that controlled the majority of today's territory of England. They waged wars often and were the last kingdom to retain paganism until their king, Penda, was killed in 655.

During their peak, Mercians held control over several important territories, some of which included former minor kingdoms. These were North and South Mercia, the so-called "outer Mercia," Lindsey, land of the Middle Angles, Hwicce, lands of the Wreocansæte, lands of the Pecsæte, the land between Ribble and Mersey, and the land of the Middle Saxons. In addition, their kings could instate puppet rulers in other larger kingdoms, asserting their dominance over them.

The Mercians would remain a powerful regional force until the rise of the West Saxons in the early 9th century. While they would remain independent during the Viking invasion, they would eventually lose their independence to Edward the Elder by the early 10th century. There were a few attempts at reinstating independence, but nothing substantial came of it. By the end of the pre-Norman period, Mercia had already been reduced to a province.

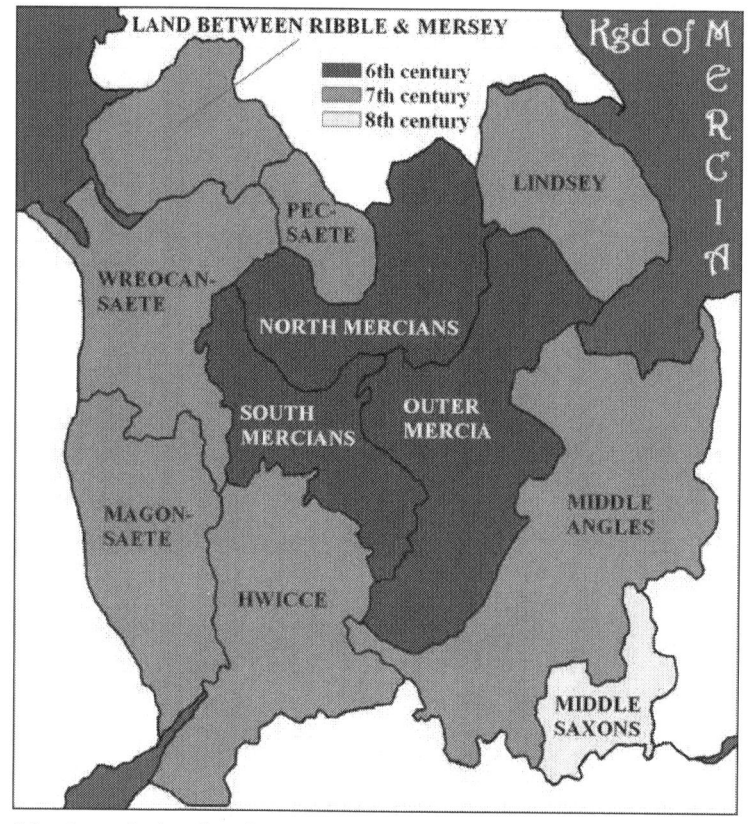

Map of Mercia at the height of its power[xii]

Notable Kings of Mercia

Penda

Penda ascended the Mercian throne probably around 626 CE. As a ruler, he was famous for his many successful campaigns against other local kings. In fact, his battles effectively ended the reigns of a few key kings from the region.

Penda's first victory came against the West Saxons when he crushed their kings Cynegils and Cwichelm at the Battle of Cirencester in 628. As a result of his victory, the West Saxon kings ceded this territory to him, which would later become part of the kingdom of Hwicce. His next major battle was the Battle of Hatfield Chase in 633, where he, together with Cadwallon, defeated Edwin of Northumbria. The alliance between Cadwallon and Penda was so fruitful that they continued with their successful campaigns well after the death of Edwin.

Oswald, the next king of Northumbria, also fell to Penda during the famous Battle of Maserfield. At this point, Penda had been ruling Mercia for at least fifteen years and had been an accomplished warlord. This is an important fact to take into consideration since Penda was still a pagan king, and Christian nations of Britain were crumbling before him left and right. In fact, it's probably safe to say that Penda would have been the last major pagan king who remained pagan until he died.

After Oswald's death, Oswiu took control of Bernicia and tried to assert himself in Deira. During this time, Penda and him had a somewhat decent relationship, and Penda even married one of his daughters to Oswiu's son Alhfrith. In addition, one of Oswiu's daughters also married one of Penda's sons, his heir apparent, Peada. However, Peada had to convert to Christianity for this marriage to happen. Despite being pagan himself, Penda apparently tolerated Christians, even going so far as to condemn those who declared themselves Christian but didn't follow the tenets of their belief.

However, none of this would stop Penda from eventually invading Oswiu's kingdom in 655. While Oswiu initially bought peace with gold, Penda still wanted to crush him. However, a combination of opportunity, military desertion of Mercian soldiers, and luck would see Oswiu attack Penda in the minor Battle of the Winwaed that same year. Penda's army was far larger, but Oswiu struck when it was most vulnerable. Penda was killed, and as a consequence, his son Peada was installed as a puppet king serving directly under Oswiu. The Northumbrian king would rule the Mercians for about three years before a new king would take the throne and establish himself as the new powerhouse of Mercia.

Wulfhere

Shortly after he was installed as a puppet king, Peada of Mercia was killed, giving Oswiu direct dominion of Mercia. However, in 658, three men named Immin, Eafa, and Eadbert rebelled against the Northumbrian king and elevated the other son of Penda as king. That son would be known as the first Christian king of Mercia, and his name was Wulfhere.

It didn't take long for Wulfhere to begin his own conquest of the southern kingdoms. He initially made an alliance with Æthelwealh of Sussex, helping him convert to Christianity. The year 661 would see Wulfhere gifting the South Saxons the Isle of Wight, which he had previously razed.

During this same year, Wulfhere attacked the West Saxons. By the 670s, he had effectively become the overlord of the region, and the Mercians would retain this power until King Cædwalla got on the counteroffensive. We also know that Wulfhere had a powerful influence in Kent, Lindsey, Surrey, Essex, and East Anglia.

But Wulfhere lost some key battles in his later years. Ecgfrith of Northumbria, for example, managed to defeat the Mercian king in 674, despite having a smaller army. Wulfhere survived the battle, however, though he lost a significant portion of territory and was forced to pay tribute to Ecgfrith. In a different battle, he faced the king of Wessex Æscwine, a mere year after losing to the Northumbrians. The result of this battle isn't known to us, but we know that Wulfhere survived it. Ultimately, the Mercian king died later that same year, probably from a disease. His brother Æthelred took the throne and even reclaimed some of the territories Wulfhere had lost, but he was nowhere near as skilled of a ruler as his predecessor.

Offa

The history of Mercia would not feel complete without Offa. Ascending to the throne in 757, this ruler was by far the most powerful Mercian king to have ever lived, and when we compare his power and influence to other Anglo-Saxon kings, he was only outshined by Alfred the Great.

During his reign, Offa would come to dominate Kent, Essex, Wessex, and East Anglia. His overlordship of Wessex came to pass in 779 after the Battle of Bensington where he defeated the West Saxon king Cynewulf. In terms of Kent, he even reduced the influence of Canterbury by establishing an archdiocese in Lichfield in 787. The only kingdom he could not influence directly was Northumbria, though the two kingdoms did arrange a few political marriages.

Offa also battled the local Britons. In fact, the Welsh kingdom of Powys had so many clashes with the Mercians that Offa ordered the construction of a massive dyke whose remains still stand today. Offa's Dyke was 65 ft. wide and 8 ft. high, and it was built in a way to both prevent the Britons from invading and to give the military a good overview of the area.

Several indicators show us how powerful Offa really was. For instance, coins were minted with his face and name during the period of his reign. In addition, a few documents even list him as *Rex Anglorum*, or the King of the English, though their historicity is not entirely certain. He even remained in frequent contact with King Charlemagne, though the monarch would turn his attention to other matters in later years.

Offa died in 796, and as he had desired, his son Ecgfrith succeeded him on the throne, though he presumably died 141 days after his ascension. Considering how frequently Offa would eliminate his dynastic rivals and how badly he wanted Ecgfrith to rule, this created a succession problem which led to a distant relative of Offa's, Cœnwulf, taking the throne.

Other Notable Kings of Mercia

Of the other Mercian kings, the most notable ones that left their mark on history are Æthelred, Æthelbald, and Cœnwulf. Æthelred had inherited the throne from Wulfhere, and as stated, he couldn't maintain a lot of influence on other kingdoms as his predecessor did. He was known as a very devout Christian, but more interestingly, he was also one of the first Mercian kings to abdicate the throne and become a priest. In 697, his queen and wife, Osthryth, the daughter of the Northumbrian king Oswiu, died under mysterious circumstances. Seven years later, Æthelred abdicated the throne and took up monastic vows in Bardney, a monastery that he had founded with Osthryth. This monastery also contains his remains.

Æthelbald ascended the Mercian throne in 716 and began his own series of conquests. Soon enough, he became the dominant force, with only Northumbria being out of his reach. During his reign, the main Anglo-Saxon missionary in Germany, Boniface, reprimanded Æthelbald for his many sins regarding his treatment of the Church. Possibly as a response to this, Æthelbald issued a charter at the synod of Gumley in 749 giving more rights and privileges to the Church. He died in 757 with the popular belief being that the murderers of this Mercian king were his own bodyguards.

Cœnwulf ruled Mercia after the death of Offa's son. He was known to have reestablished Mercian overlordship in several kingdoms, as evidenced by coins with his face minted there. He was also known for his apparent clash with Wulfred, the Archbishop of Canterbury. Apparently, the archbishop and the king disagreed on the matter of laypeople controlling churches and monasteries. This could have possibly resulted in Wulfred losing the right to perform his priestly duties for at least four years. When Cœnwulf died in 821, the overlordship of Mercia ended, and there would be no other ruler from this kingdom to exercise such power ever again.

Wessex

Out of all the kingdoms, the one ruled by the West Saxons held out the longest. At first, the West Saxons didn't take up a lot of territory in Britain, being situated between Sussex to the east and the kingdom of Dumnonia to the west. Their story begins, according to legend, when Kings Cerdic and Cynric landed in 495 on British soil. By the late 6th century, Wessex was already an established kingdom, and it was very active in political affairs. The second king to be named bretwalda by Bede and the *Anglo-Saxon Chronicle* was Ceawlin of Wessex who probably ruled between 560 and 592, though we know precious little about him.

During the rise of both Mercia and Northumbria as local political powerhouses, Wessex remained a semi-independent kingdom, at one time falling under direct Mercian control. However, after Cædwalla's ascension to the throne, Wessex grew in strength and size, slowly becoming an important political player on the island. It was the house of Wessex that would later be the dominant force in Britain by uniting the kingdoms, fending off the Danes, and founding the first English dynasty of kings. This dynasty would be deposed and reinstated several times, with the Danish kings controlling the isle at a few points during this period. Without a doubt, Wessex would rise to be the most important of the seven kingdoms, having been the progenitors of the idea of a unified Britain long before William conquered the island.

Notable Kings of Wessex

Cædwalla

Cædwalla's name is likely Celtic in origin, but his actions very much impacted the Anglo-Saxons around him. After years in exile, Cædwalla attacked Sussex with a small army and killed their king, Æthelwealh, with possible help from Bishop Wilfrid. However, he was driven out of Sussex by the late king's ealdormen. This didn't stop the West Saxon king from attempting to conquer other kingdoms, though. Soon after that, either in 685 or 686, he became king of Wessex. With his newfound power, he conquered the Isle of Wight and, if some sources are to be believed, killed the local Jutish population, which would make this the first proper genocide in the history of Britain. Not long after his campaign in Wight, Cædwalla went after Kent, deposing their ruler and installing Mul as king. However, Mul was burned by the Kentish soon after, so Cædwalla more than likely ruled this kingdom directly afterward.

Cædwalla himself wasn't Christian at the time, but he was on the fast track to becoming one. While on Wight, he demanded the locals convert, and their refusal to do so might have been the catalyst for their extermination at the hands of the West Saxon king. It was during this battle that Cædwalla sustained serious injuries. As a consequence of this, he abdicated the throne in 688 in favor of his successor and distant cousin Ine. After abdicating, Cædwalla went to Rome to get himself baptized. He reached it a year later, and ten days after his baptism took place, he died a proper Christian.

Ine

Ine ascended the throne of Wessex in 688 after Cædwalla's abdication. During his reign, he made peace with Kent, continued the subjugation of the South Saxons, and held control over Surrey and Essex. He was also known to have led campaigns against the Celtic kingdom of Dumnonia and even had clashes with the Mercians, though we do not know the results of these battles.

Ine's reign saw the economic rise and expansion of the settlement named Hamwic, which would later become part of today's Southampton. Trade was frequent in this town, and people would exchange glass vessels and animal hides. There were even imported goods and foreign currency from mainland Europe found in this town. From what we can ascertain, the town housed over 5,000 people, which was a massive number for a settlement at the time. Ine was also the first West Saxon ruler to issue coin minting, though this can't be proven with archeological evidence since the sceattas usually didn't bear names or faces of contemporary kings.

Like Cædwalla, Ine also abdicated the throne, and he did so in 726, leaving no clear heir to the throne. With his wife, Queen Æthelburg, he again mirrored the previous king by traveling to Rome. However, unlike Cædwalla, Ine had already been converted during his reign. It is possible, however, that he founded the *Schola Saxonum*, an institution for West Saxon pilgrims, in Italy, which later English Christians would visit for various religious reasons.

Ine was not only a skilled warrior and a devout Christian, but he was also a lawmaker, as evidence suggests he might have drafted his own code of law at the same time as Wihtred of Kent, though Ine made his code public in 694.

Ecgberht

Ecgberht, another king to start his life in exile, would forever be remembered as the king who annihilated Mercian supremacy over the other kingdoms. He became king of Wessex in 802 and maintained independence from Mercia. In his early years, his ealdormen had to face the forces of Mercia-dominated Hwicce, which ended in the deaths of the ealdormen on both sides but a victory for Wessex nonetheless. The king of Mercia at the time was Offa's successor, Cœnwulf. From what we know, he didn't rule over Wessex, and Ecgberht maintained his independence, though he didn't have a lot of outside influence at first.

Ecgberht's military efforts earned him his first success in Dumnonia. Later, in 825, the West Saxon king would face off against Beornwulf of Mercia at the decisive Battle of Ellandun. Immediately after the battle, according to the *Anglo-Saxon Chronicle*, Ecgberht's son, Æthelwulf, managed to subjugate Kent, Sussex, Essex, and Surrey. Beornwulf likely attacked the West Saxon forces first, but with the combined efforts of several Anglo-Saxon armies, he was defeated completely, though he didn't perish. However, he was more or less emasculated by the loss, and he tried to invade East Anglia the next year only to end up slain. His successor, Ludeca, was also slain by the East Angles in 827, and by 829, Ecgberht had invaded Mercia and driven their king into exile. At this point, Ecgberht effectively held power over nearly all of the Anglo-Saxon kingdoms, excluding Northumbria. However, the Mercians regained their independence under Wiglaf the next year, though they didn't have nearly as much influence as before.

Ecgberht continued fighting, losing a battle against the Danes in 836 at Carthampton but beating them and their Dumnonian allies two years later at the Battle of Hingston Down. This effectively ended the independence of Cornish Britons, a people group native to the South West Peninsula of Britain, though their royal line continued to exist sometime after this.

Ecgberht died in 839 and was buried in Winchester, as would his descendants years later. According to his will, he left his kingdom and his estates to the male members of his family.

Alfred the Great

Alfred was possibly the greatest ruler of Wessex and really all of the Anglo-Saxon kingdoms before the Norman invasion. He ascended the throne in 871 as the king of the West Saxons, but in 886, he would come to be styled as the king of the Anglo-Saxons. During his reign, the Danes became an increasing threat, and during the first seven years of his reign, Alfred was not doing very well against them. The Danes kept pressing onward, forcing Alfred to negotiate peace and pay them off on more than a few occasions. At one point, the Danes, led by Guthrum, attacked Chippenham in 878, forcing Alfred to flee. After this, most of the Anglo-Saxon kingdoms were now under Danish rule.

However, Alfred would not take this lying down. Later that year, he would rally his forces and crush Guthrum's defenses at the Battle of Edington. He would then push the Danes all the way to Chippenham and starved them until they caved. Once Guthrum surrendered, the two rulers negotiated peace terms. The Danish king had to convert to

Christianity, which he did alongside 29 trusted chieftains. Moreover, Mercia was divided between the two kings, and Guthrum was to retain only sections of East Anglia, with this new kingdom of his being called the Danelaw. Alfred hadn't liberated all of the Anglo-Saxon kingdoms, but he had managed to sufficiently hurt the Danes and reduce their influence.

Though the Danes had been beaten, some Viking raids were still taking place during Alfred's reign. However, no large-scale warfare took place for some time. In 886, Alfred retook London and made it into a habitable town again. It's this year, and possibly even the result of this event, that saw the king of Wessex declared king of all Anglo-Saxons, though Alfred himself never used that title.

After the death of Guthrum, the lack of a clear successor threatened another war with the Danes, and after 892, they began to strike again. However, after a series of battles such as those at Farnham, Benfleet, and Buttington, the Danes more or less retreated either to Danelaw or to continental Europe.

Alfred was known as a lot more than just a skilled warrior. He was probably the most literate king to have ever ruled Wessex, having translated a number of important works. He also placed great emphasis on vernacular English language rather than on Latin. Moreover, he founded a court school where he wanted to see his children, other nobles, and even intelligent low-born children learn how to read and write. Naturally, he was extremely interested in religion and had maintained good relations with Rome, even receiving a piece of the "true cross" from Pope Marinus in 883, though there's not a lot of agreement about this event among the scholars.

Alfred would die in October 899 and would be succeeded by his son Edward the Elder. Like his father before him, Edward would be a great king, venerated by the Church and loved by the Anglo-Saxon people. His title would also be the king of Anglo-Saxons, but it wouldn't be him that would unite the island.

Commemorative statue of Alfred the Great, Winchester [xiii]

Æthelstan

In 924, after Edward's death, Æthelstan took the Anglo-Saxon throne. However, he wasn't the heir to the throne; his younger brother Ælfweard had ruled for a little over two weeks, dying soon after. Æthelstan would first act only as a Mercian king, considering most nobles saw him as unfit and illegitimate to succeed to the throne. However, he was crowned king anyway in 925 at the place called Kingston upon Thames.

Æthelstan's early years saw him fighting the Danes. After a strategic marriage of his sister to Sihtric, the Viking king, and his subsequent death, Æthelstan saw the opportunity to attack the Danes. He captured York in 927, beating Sihtric's successor, Guthfrith. A year later, several northern kings accepted Æthelstan as their overlord. At long last, the Anglo-Saxon lands north of Humber were part of the greater English territory, though Æthelstan would not be well liked by his new northern subjects since he was a southern invader. Æthelstan's next successful campaign took him south where he fully subjugated the Cornish and established a new episcopal see, the area of a bishop's ecclesiastical jurisdiction. The year 927 would be one of great victories for Æthelstan, and it would also see him don a new title, that of King of the English.

But it wasn't any of these events that cemented the former Anglo-Saxon king as one of the greatest of his time. It was the event that took place a decade later that would not only give Æthelstan more well-earned recognition, but it would also be the cornerstone of English nationalism. Namely, in 934, the king of the Anglo-Saxons decided to invade Scotland for unspecified reasons. The results of the ensuing battles weren't recorded, but the Scots didn't sit still. Soon after, in 937, an alliance of three kings, Olaf Guthfrithson of Dublin, Constantine II of Alba, today's Scotland, and Owen of Strathclyde, faced Æthelstan in the Battle of Brunanburh. Despite suffering great losses, Æthelstan crushed his opponents, with some of them fleeing and their armies scattering. At that point, England fought as a single entity against a disunited foe and won.

Two years later, Æthelstan died in Gloucester. Aside from his military victories, he is also remembered as a learned man who invested a lot of time and money in the church and education, just like his father and grandfather before him. After his death, the control of the land would shift between his heirs and the Danes, though neither of the two dynasties would end up the victor after the events of the Battle of Hastings in 1066.

Other Notable Kings of Wessex

The Wessex line continued well after Æthelstan, but in terms of kings before the title King of the English existed, the two that absolutely should be mentioned are Cynewulf and Edward the Elder.

Cynewulf followed his predecessor Sigeberht and took the throne in 757. With the death of the Mercian king Æthelbald, he took the opportunity of the political turmoil in that kingdom and asserted Wessex's independence. A series of wars would grant him victories over the Mercians and the Welsh, cementing the status of Wessex at the time. While he might have been defeated by Offa of Mercia at the Battle of Bensington, he never really became his subject, remaining an independent king. Cynewulf's reign ended with him being killed by Sigeberht's brother, Cyneheard the Ætheling, in front of Cynewulf's own ealdormen and thegns, though this story might be apocryphal.

The story of Edward the Elder, on the other hand, is the story of a capable king inheriting the throne of his equally capable father, Alfred. In 917 and early 918, Edward conquered the south of Danelaw and made it a part of his unified Anglo-Saxon kingdom. Of course, the Danish wouldn't cease their activities after these defeats and would continue to play key political roles in the years to come, even after Edward's successors followed on the English throne. Edward himself died in Farndon in 924, after successfully squashing the rebellions of the Mercians and the Welsh.

Chapter 6 – Anglo-Saxon Legacy

Though archeological evidence is not as abundant as we'd need it to be to have a clearer picture of Anglo-Saxon societies, we can safely say that they left a decent mark on European history. The willingness to convert to Christianity by some of the earlier kings gave the people their first written works, as well as the basis for early legal texts considering how their codes included a lot of Christian tenets. But the Anglo-Saxon Christians themselves had a massive influence on the continental Christians. Their missions would ultimately lead to conversions of many pagan tribes in Saxony, Scandinavia, and other parts of Central Europe.

In addition, the royal families of Europe took notice of these kingdoms, and very early on, there were different types of relations between them. Not only did the kings intermarry and share military campaigns, but trade was booming, and in time, individual kings started to form proper countries that were nothing like the Roman provinces that used to take up the island.

The relationship between the Anglo-Saxons and Rome, in particular, was very prolific. Popes would frequently gift the monarchs of various Anglo-Saxon kingdoms with holy gifts, and monarchs would visit Rome for either pilgrimages or baptisms.

However, their biggest legacy came from the earlier efforts of unification. Namely, Britain had been a country of far more than seven kingdoms. Local Britons, Scots, and Picts, as well as Danish Vikings later on and various other people groups, all had minor kingdoms and territories within the isle, and these petty kingdoms kept vying for one form of supremacy or another. But as early as the 6th century, certain kings began showing signs of wanting to unify the lands of the Angles, the Saxons, and the Jutes. Æthelstan would accomplish this unification, though it would still be on shaky ground after his death. Nevertheless, an idea of a unified England had been set in stone during those days, and the very idea of being English has remained strong to this very day.

The Anglo-Saxon legacy can also be seen in their treatment of women and their art. For instance, not a lot of societies in early medieval Europe would allow women to hold power within the Church. However, that was not the case with Kent and subsequent Christian kingdoms where women of noble birth could become abbesses or nuns. And regarding art, Anglo-Saxon illuminated manuscripts influenced many different Christian art styles in Central and Western Europe, and it was thanks to its blend of traditional Anglo-Saxon, and even Celtic, elements and the typical Christian motifs found in Italy.

By far, the greatest legacy the Anglo-Saxon rulers left to their subjects was the emphasis on vernacular English being used in church sermons, as well as the importance of translating books from Latin to Old English. This gave the people of Britain more independence from the main Church in Rome, and it got the laity closer to the priestly class. This decision would also lead to an expansion of Anglo-Saxon literature which would give us secular accounts of the period and a massive wealth of historical information that came first-hand from the authors who lived back then.

Frontispiece of Bede's Life of St. Cuthbert; King Æthelstan is giving a copy of the book to the saint[xiv]

Conclusion

It's indeed odd to think that raiders and settlers from a few minor Germanic tribes in today's Germany and Denmark would not only settle an island well off their coasts but that they would also go on to establish kingdoms, convert to Christianity and later spread it across the continent, do successful trades with others, forge alliances with bigger kingdoms in Western and Central Europe, crush the local populace, and even undergo a massive unification. It's also odd to think that this same island, with these same settlers, would one day become a massive united kingdom which would dominate a quarter of the people and land of the world. History is anything but boring, and if we look at the Anglo-Saxons and their near seven-century history in Britain, we can tell just how insane and unpredictable it can really be.

But it's not just about the Anglo-Saxons turning from pagans to Christians and from being the dominated to the dominant. It's a far bigger tale than that. After all, these people left us with an entirely new culture forged from several different sources. They left us with a mix of Roman heritage, Celtic influences, Anglo-Saxon customs and beliefs, and Christian culture, all of it resulting in a unique social phenomenon. Their lives on the island of Britain had gone through many shifts. They saw their language change and adapt, their beliefs shift and grow, their art becoming unlike anything they had done before on the continent, and their relations with others strained but not strained enough to refuse unification when it finally arrived.

Britain is home to some of the greatest figures in collective human history. However, this was a trend well before England existed as a country. Kent would produce a lot of learned bishops as would Northumbria years later. Kings would turn from tribal warlords to learned, well-read men who were pious to a fault but fierce with a sword. Mercia, Northumbria, and Wessex would offer historians dozens of kings whose reigns included massive conquests and equally dreadful losses. And ultimately, the very term "Anglo-Saxon," which likely meant nothing when Angles, Saxons, and Jutes landed on the shores of Britain those many centuries ago, had at one point represented a clear term of identification for many. The Anglo-Saxons were, in a sense, a bit of an accident, but it would be an accident that would give birth to a thousand years of history that would affect all of Europe and, indeed, the rest of the world.

Free Bonus from Captivating History (Available for a Limited time)

Hi History Lovers!

Now you have a chance to join our exclusive history list so you can get your first history ebook for free as well as discounts and a potential to get more history books for free! Simply visit the link below to join.

Captivatinghistory.com/ebook

Also, make sure to follow us on Facebook, Twitter and Youtube by searching for Captivating History.

Bibliography and References

Medieval Chronicles™ (2014). Retrieved on March 11th 2019, from http://www.medievalchronicles.com

Encyclopaedia Britannica (1981), Retrieved on March 11th 2019, from https://www.britannica.com

Fell, C. (1986): *Women in Anglo-Saxon England*. Oxford, UK: Basil Blackwell Ltd.

Gomme, E.E.C (1909): *The Anglo-Saxon Chronicle, Newly Translated by E.E.C. Gomme, B.A.* London, UK: George Bell and Sons

Higham, N. J. (2015): *The Anglo-Saxon World*. New Haven, Ct, USA & London, UK: Yale University Press

Stanley, E.G. (2000): *Imagining the Anglo-Saxon Past: The Search for Anglo-Saxon Paganism and Anglo-Saxon Trial by Jury*. Cambridge, UK: D. S. Brewer

Magennis, H. (1996): *Images of Community in Old English Poetry*. Cambridge, UK: Cambridge University Press

Wikipedia (January 15, 2001), Retrieved on March 11th 2019, from https://www.wikipedia.org/

Yorke, B. (1990): *Kings and Kingdoms of Early Anglo-Saxon England.* New York, NY, USA & London, UK: Routledge

Notes on Images

[i] Original image uploaded by Lotroo, on 19 February 2013. Retrieved from https://commons.wikimedia.org on March 2019 under the following license: Public Domain. This item is in the public domain, and can be used, copied, and modified without any restrictions.

[ii] Original image uploaded by Notuncurious on 25 January 2013. Retrieved from https://commons.wikimedia.org/ on March 2019 with minor modifications under the following license: Creative Commons Attribution-Share Alike 3.0 Unported. This license lets others remix, tweak, and build upon your work even for commercial reasons, as long as they credit you and license their new creations under the identical terms.

[iii] Original image uploaded by Hoodinski, on 23 March 2011. Retrieved from https://commons.wikimedia.org on March 2019 under the following license: Public Domain. This item is in the public domain, and can be used, copied, and modified without any restrictions.

[iv] Original image uploaded by geni on 28 December 2016. Retrieved from https://commons.wikimedia.org/ on March 2019 with minor modifications under the following license: Creative Commons Attribution-Share Alike 4.0 International. This license lets others remix, tweak, and build upon your work even for commercial reasons, as long as they credit you and license their new creations under the identical terms.

[v] Original image uploaded by Oosoom on 3 August 2009. Retrieved from https://commons.wikimedia.org/ on March 2019 with minor modifications under the following license: Creative Commons Attribution-Share Alike 3.0 Unported. This license lets others remix, tweak, and build upon your work even for commercial reasons, as long as they credit you and license their new creations under the identical terms.

[vi] Original image uploaded by geni on 23 May 2014. Retrieved from https://commons.wikimedia.org/ on March 2019 with minor modifications under the following license: Creative Commons Attribution-Share Alike 4.0 International. This license lets others remix, tweak, and build upon your work even for commercial reasons, as long as they credit you and license their new creations under the identical terms.

[vii] Original image uploaded by The Yorck Project, on 20 May 2005. Retrieved from https://commons.wikimedia.org on March 2019 under the following license: Public Domain. This item is in the public domain, and can be used, copied, and modified without any restrictions.

[viii] Original image uploaded by GDK, on 22 August 2005. Retrieved from https://commons.wikimedia.org on March 2019 under the following license: Public Domain. This item is in the public domain, and can be used, copied, and modified without any restrictions.

[ix] Original image uploaded by Polylerus on 24 June 2006. Retrieved from https://commons.wikimedia.org/ on March 2019 with minor modifications under the following license: Creative Commons Attribution-Share Alike 3.0 Unported. This license lets others remix, tweak, and build upon your work even for commercial reasons, as long as they credit you and license their new creations under the identical terms.

[x] Original image uploaded by Hel-hama on 22 July 2012. Retrieved from https://commons.wikimedia.org/ on March 2019 with minor modifications under the following license: Creative Commons Attribution-Share Alike 3.0 Unported. This license lets others remix, tweak, and build upon your work even for commercial reasons, as long as they credit you and license their new creations under the identical terms.

[xi] Original image uploaded by Thomas Gun on 31 October 2009. Retrieved from https://commons.wikimedia.org/ on March 2019 with minor modifications under the following license: *Creative Commons Attribution-ShareAlike 2.0 Generic.* This license lets others remix, tweak, and build upon your work even for commercial reasons, as long as they credit you and license their new creations under the identical terms.

[xii] Original image uploaded by TharkunColl on 9 September 2009. Retrieved from https://commons.wikimedia.org/ on March 2019 with minor modifications under the following license: Creative Commons Attribution-Share Alike 3.0. This license lets others remix, tweak, and build upon your work even for commercial reasons, as long as they credit you and license their new creations under the identical terms.

[xiii] Original image uploaded by Odejea on 25 August 2005. Retrieved from https://commons.wikimedia.org/ on March 2019 with minor modifications under the following license: Creative Commons Attribution-Share Alike 3.0 Unported. This license lets others remix, tweak, and build upon your work even for

commercial reasons, as long as they credit you and license their new creations under the identical terms.

[xiv] Original image uploaded by Soerfm, on 12 July 2018. Retrieved from https://commons.wikimedia.org on March 2019 under the following license: Public Domain. This item is in the public domain, and can be used, copied, and modified without any restrictions.

Made in the USA
Lexington, KY
30 July 2019